MW00629792

12-10-91
God Bless You

POEMS
of the
HEART

Original Works
by R. Douglas Veer

Changed Lives Publishing, LLC

2021

Poetry Contained Herein are Original Works
Copyright © 2021 By R. Douglas Veer
Permission for the use of
these poems and Scripture verses
is hereby granted for personal use,
with gratitude by the author.

First Printing: 2021
ISBN-13: 978-1-7323243-2-9
Library of Congress Control Number: 2021902537

Cover Design: K. Veer
Front & Back Cover Graphic: iStock.com:
Autumn style vector. Russia, Design, Frame-Border,
September, Square-Composition

* * *

Book Ordering: Amazon.com
Booking Information, please contact:
DVM@DougVeer.com or visit
www.KathyVeer.com and www.DougVeer.com

Changed Lives Publishing, LLC
Region of Augusta, Georgia

YOUR OPINION COUNTS!

If you have enjoyed
this book,
please consider
writing a short
book review
at Amazon.com

Help us spread the word,
and share Jesus
with others too!

TABLE OF CONTENTS

"If it's somewhere in a heart . . . it's somewhere in a poem."
R Douglas Veer

A POEM

❧ ❧ ❧

Oh, how the mighty hand of God
created everything.
The trees, the flowers, the flowing brooks,
the birds, and every song they sing.

He gave us stars to light the night
and a sun to warm the day.
And then to guide us through the dark
He made a moon to light our way.

Oh, how His wonders do surround us
if we'll but take the time to see
how beautiful He made His world
to share with you and me.

Yes, flowers, birds, and dewdrops too
with songs that only they can sing
created He, to bless us with
a world which only He could bring.

But as He watched His final work,
the woman and the man,
created He, our wondrous God,
a gift, as only His love can.

Within the breathing breast He put
a heart, like His alone.
And there within the heart God wrote
for it to speak, a poem.

And with the tender words of love
that only He, God, could impart,
created He, this tender gift,
His *poems of the heart.*

A TASTE OF BEAUTY

❧ ❧ ❧

So flocks the brilliant butterfly
upon the gentle stem
which holds the nectar of the dainty flower.

As silently, invisibly
doth beat the gentle wing
suspending it with tireless, gentle power.

Who but a God of wonders would
create one such as this
to give the world, a taste of beauty such,

that in His love for man would He
share such a majesty
to show the wonder of His love for us.

HEARTSONG MELODY

To Kathy . . . my bride to be . . .

❧ ❧ ❧

I hear the whispers in the wind
when even' tide is near,
as with its soft melodious voice
it calls the moon, "Come hear."

I hear the gurbling of the brook
as it comes trippling down,
across the rocky meadow's face
with wrinkles in its brow.

I hear the branches of the pines
play syncopated rustling tunes,
that harmonize with evening doves
and owls and lutes and loons.

Then as the brook and wing and wind
join in the orchestrated mewl,
the night, alive with moon and stars
is suddenly born anew

Soon, love's crescendo booms and cries
in catalytic swoon,
as hearts unite "en musicale"
beneath a lover's moon.

And then in soft melodic notes,
your love song comes to me,
and matches melody and rhyme
to my own *"Heartsong Melody."*

SHADOW ON THE WALL

❧ ❧ ❧

When I go into my secret prayer room
it's a peaceful place to be.
The Holiness of God, shines there
so brilliantly on me.
And in His presence I forget
all my worldly cares.
I get to be His shadow on the wall.

Oh, if I could share the feeling,
of how it is when I bow there.
How His eyes are like cool fire,
and the sun melts in His hair.
Golden moments spent with Jesus;
there is nothing can compare.
He's my Savior;
I'm His shadow on the wall.

Bathing in His presence there,
'til the moon is out of sight.
The daystar blinks its warning,
of the coming morning light.
So, I rise in full surrender,
where His presence has made me
humbly His;
His blessed shadow on the wall.

So I go into my secret prayer room,
it's a peaceful place to be.
The Holiness of God, shines there . . .
so brilliantly on me.
And in His presence I forget,
all my worldly cares.
I get to be His shadow on the wall.

DADDY'S GIRL

❧ ❧ ❧

There are a lot of things to think about
in this ole crazy world
Especially when you're *Daddy*
to a precious "baby girl".
You think about the "whooping cough"
and "mumps" and "measles" too,
and wonder,
"If she get's them, whatever will I do?"

But somehow she comes through those years
and learns to crawl and walk.
And then one day you hear, "Daddy,"
as she begins to talk!
With every year that passes by
your heart swells more and more,
as patiently you watch with pride
for what God has in store.

She goes to school and does real well
and you're so pleased for her,
as you watch her grow up to be
a precious "teen-age" girl.

And now you know that soon she'll be
a woman . . . and you pray,
that she will give her heart to God,
before some boy takes it away.

But she will never leave your mind
and surely not your heart,
because deep down within your soul
she'll always be a part.
Dear daughter, YOU . . . "light up my life,"
so please never forget
that whether you are young or old
you'll always be, "Daddy's girl," yet.

GIFT TO A SON

❧ ❧ ❧

Take a boy; give him a bike,
a big red ball or anything.
Yet while you're giving don't forget
to give to him a day.

A day when he can be alone
to do as he wants to do.
Lay 'neath a tree and watch the sky
as the clouds travel over the blue.

A day to go down to the creek
and get his clothing wet,
while knowing deep inside that surely
you won't be upset.

And then before you notice he
will become a man who will say,
"Son, here's the greatest gift I have."
And he'll give to him a day.

THE CROSS IN MY POCKET

❧ ❧ ❧

I carry a cross in my pocket;
a simple reminder to me
that I am a Christian,
no matter where I may be.

This little cross isn't magic,
nor is it a good luck charm.
It isn't meant to protect me
from every physical harm.

It's not for identification
for all the world to see.
It's simply an understanding
between my Savior and me.

When I put my hand in my pocket
to bring out a coin or a key,
the cross is there to remind me
of the price He paid for me.

It reminds me, too, to be thankful
for my blessings every day,
and to strive to serve Him better
in all that I do or say.

It's also a daily reminder
of the peace and comfort I share
with all who know my Master
and give themselves to His care.

So, I carry a cross in my pocket
reminding none but me
that Jesus Christ is Lord of my life,
if I will let Him be.

IN MEMORY OF . . .

❧ ❧ ❧

Our table was set poorly;
our shoes were thin and bare.
The winds blew cold upon our heads
protected just by hair.
The clothes we wore were patch on patch
from years of hand-me-downs.
Yes, we were the poorest of the poor
that lived here in this town.
The rich kids sneered and laughed at us;
the poor kids turned their backs.
'Cause we came from the "Organ Factory"
down by the railroad tracks.
But Daddy always worked each day
so we could learn the same.
And he was never shamed like me
when he said, "Veer's my name."
And as the years went on
I could see that Daddy gave me pride,
and taught me honesty, and trust,
and compassion too, besides.
He taught me strength and warmth and love
and kindness for the weak.
He taught me to know right from wrong
and showed me how to seek . . .
. . . the richer things that life can give,
to those who take the time
to search out and to reach for life
instead of being blind,
to all the goodness that there is;
to reap, as we love on,
instead of reaching for money
and what to spend it on.
Yes, our table was set poorly;
our shoes were thin and bare.
But Daddy fed us love and kindness
and we grew, with food to spare.
Food of love and decency
that we can give to all.
That's why our Daddy's table made us grow
to be ten feet tall.

'TWAS THE FRIGHT BEFORE CHRISTMAS

A message from Joey

❧ ❧ ❧

'Twas the night before Christmas
and nobody came;
just him sitting alone
in the darkness again.
He had drank all day long
and the bottle was dry,
so with a drunken decision
he thought he'd just die.

He climbed up the stairs
to the railing above,
tied on the rope
and gave it a tug.
He looked at the clock:
eleven-twenty-two,
and thought, "It's just as well.
Yeah, it's the thing to do."

There was no one to live for.
His family didn't care
that he sat many nights
all alone in his chair.
And trying to explain to them
never worked out,
'cause they would just curse him
with loud angry shouts.

"You're just lazy, you're worthless,
a no good ole drunk.
Yeah, I listened one time.
Your excuses all stunk!

Lots of people have troubles;
lots of people have pain,
but I don't want to hear
your excuses again."

Well, they just don't care
that I miss him so much.
Once he went into battle,
we simply lost touch.
The last thing I heard was
that the enemy came,
and they caught him and beat him
while calling him names."

"Hey soldier. Hey warrior!
Hey *Johnny-Do-Good.*
If you're really so tough,
stand and fight like you should."

But they said that he wouldn't;
they said he refused,
so they gave him some more
of that awful abuse.
They removed all his clothes
and beat him some more,
'til he didn't hardly look
like Joey no more.

They beat him all the way
to the top of the hill.
There was murder in their hearts.
They wanted to kill.
So they tied up his hands
and they murdered him there,
and most of them watching
just didn't care.

Yeah, they took my son's life
on that cold battlefield,
and I can't fight this hate in my heart;
it's my shield.

So, tomorrow,
Christmas is coming again,
and there's no one to talk to,
I don't have a friend.

As I drop to my knees
and the tears start to fall,
I see a big shadow
against my bare wall.

Then something frightening
begins to appear.
And my hair stands on end
with a cold chilling fear.
What? The shadow is moving.
It's reaching for me!
It's reaching to hold me
on it's bended knee.

I've never been so drunk
that shadows could talk,
and I've never seen one
that could stand up and walk.
But you're real.
You're not shadowy.
You're touching me!
And I hear gentle words
that you're starting to speak.

What? You've lost a Son also?
They beat Him to death?
He died with two others
on the Skulls ugly crest?

And You say that Your Son
was Your joy and Your pride,
so You know how the hurt
could cause hatred inside.

What? You say I don't need to
be acting like this?
That's what everyone else
always tries to insist.

You say that Your Son died
to take care of mine?
He was with my boy Joey,
behind enemy lines?

And He died, so when Joey
was killed he could go
up to Heaven, instead of
to Hell down below?
And He knows all about
what Joey went through?
And He brought back the story
and told it to You?

Yes, the story was told
that Joey asked them to pray,
because *he* wasn't really
their enemy that day.
And he told them that inside,
they all were the same,
and the killing and fighting
was a terrible shame.

One enemy soldier
came back with this tale:
"Joey's face kept smiling
although bleeding and pale,
and he said, 'This is war',
so you'll do what you'll do,
but I want you to know,
that I'm forgiving you."

Then the soldier laid down
his weapons of war,
and declared,
"I'm not going to kill anymore.
I've just seen the death
of real Special Man,
and I'll find how to be
just like Him, if I can."

So my boy Joey died,
but he died without fear,
and that's why I've suffered
these last seven years.

Then a comfort came over
my pain-ridden heart,
and a peace in my soul
was beginning to start.

It flowed across me
like drifts in the snow,
and the wall once again
played the shadowy show.

Then just before leaving
He told me the name
of His son . . .
"It's Jesus . . . and that's why I came.
Here's a present for you,
it is sent from My Son.
It's yours if you want it.
It's called 'Salvation'."

As He left me He took
all my pain and my sins,
and a new sense of love,
peace, and joy settled in.

No, I no longer need
the gin bottle now,
because God came to me
and He showed me how
that when Christmas is near
it reminds me of hope,
'cause He tied a big "not"
in the "end of my rope."

There's a new kind of Spirit
now that I'm drinking in.
And it's not from a bottle
of whiskey or gin.
It's called Jesus . . . and Joey . . .
in Heaven above.
So, "Merry Christmas, to you all,
with all of my love."

SAIL ON, OLD SHIP OF ZION

❧ ❧ ❧

She's a big old ship
and she's sitting mighty low in the water
'cause she's been on her maiden voyage
ever since the blood of Calvary bought her.

She's weathered many violent storms
tho' some passengers jumped overboard and drowned,
but she's not just some Titanic;
she's the beautiful Church and she ain't goin' down

Sail on, old ship of Zion.
Brave what lurks in the cold dark night.
Sail on, old ship of Zion
'till you see that beacon light.
Sail on, old ship of Zion.
He's on board . . . you're not alone.
Sail on 'til you hear the Captain say,
"Land is in sight; you've made it home."

This ship was launched from a hill outside Jerusalem
where it caught a brand new gust of wind
when she breezed through the upper room.
She rode out a storm with a jail cell song at midnight
what makes you think she's gonna sink
in some modern day typhoon?
Sail on, old ship of Zion.
He's on board . . . you're not alone.
Sail on 'til you hear the Captain say,
"Land is in sight; you've made it home."

Sail on, old ship of Zion.
Sail on, old ship of Zion.
Sail on, old ship of Zion.
The Captain is on board
and we'll soon hear the Him say,
"Come on into port, Church,
you've safely made it home."

TOUCHED BY THE MASTER'S HAND

❧ ❧ ❧

We live, we cry, we laugh, we die.
It happens all too soon.
No sooner does the sun arise,
it's time to kiss the moon.

The winter snow, the summer heat,
the Indian summer rains.
No sooner is it time to plant,
then harvest comes again.

We're born, we live, but does our life
perform what's to be done?
Or are we just a wooden bell
that never does get rung?

Oh just to be a butterfly
that has fulfilled its task
to go from worm to wing-ed grace
because the Lord has asked,
that it relinquish all its rights
into His guiding hand,
and then perform what e'er He says
because it understands,
that God has marked it from its birth
when it was but a worm,
to be a gorgeous butterfly
to beautify the Earth.

From life, to death, to life again;
from worm to butterfly,
to be thus marked and used of God,
so there in dreams go I.

Oh, just to be obedient
unto the hand of God,
and make a mark for Him alone
as o'er this earth I trod.

Oh but from birth to death to live
and fully understand,
that there has been a mark on me
placed by the Master's hand.

Hardly is a life worthwhile,
beginning to the end,
unless it finishes the race
by knowing God as friend.

So touch me God and make it true
though I am just a man,
but touched, and marked, and set aside;
marked for Your master plan.

Marked for Your use what e'er it be
though eons of time pass by;
marked as the beauty of the worm
that is Your butterfly.

A birth, a child, a man, a dream,
I pray you'll understand,
that life is meaningless until
it's touched by the Master's hand.

ON BEHALF OF LAUREN DEAN

Written for my good friends
Richard and Doreen Dean
in loving memory of their daughter
Lauren Dean

❧ ❧ ❧

Dear Richard and Doreen . . .

I know you woke up this morning,
expecting Lauren to be in her bed.
Your throat choked back on the crying,
remembering she was gone instead
of being where you always woke her,
with rumpled bedding and dark tousled hair.
You sat and touched where she should be,
as if you could still feel her there.

But remember that God in His goodness
has given a new place to rest.
Now she snuggles her face when she's tired
on the Savior's strong, peaceful chest.

Her aches and her hurts are all over.
She'll never know sickness again.
The struggles she knew in this world
are over; they've all come to an end.

Although she's with Jesus forever,
and you know everything is alright,
it's okay if you cry on her pillow,
because she won't be there tonight.

But the morning is coming when you'll go
to bed and you won't speak her name,
and when you do, please be happy;
this is healing . . . so don't be ashamed.

You see, healing is needed, and coming,
so that God can give back memories
of the joy that you felt on the mornings
when you'd go and awake her from sleep.

This mystery one day will be over,
and we'll know what she knows now,
that God in his infinite mercy
has never once broken a vow.

He's the God that created the mornings
and the God that created the night,
and He's with Lauren each moment
though for you, she's just out of sight.

So, remember that your day is coming
when His promises Jesus will keep,
and Lauren will be there one morning
with a kiss to wake *you* from *your* sleep.

WHAT HAVE I SUFFERED FOR JESUS?

❧ ❧ ❧

Listening to the rush of living,
bouncing from each street and wall.
Laughter shouting all around me,
'til I'm filled with such appall.
Raucous, loud, and rowdy laughter,
abandon, giddiness, and more,
travels through the air around me,
like a mighty rushing roar.

So I walk, not as the others
as they dance in gay sunshine,
tasting all the worldly pleasures
while mine is quiet and sublime.
Why do *they* drink in the good life?
Why do *they* have all there is?
While so sadly I pass by them,
without knowing that I wish
I could have the fun as they do
and would dare to be so perk.
No, my 'P's and Q's' I must watch,
'cause I suffer to go to church.

Rising up each Sunday morning,
I get dressed; head out the door,
and I quietly sit and listen.
Another sermon (sigh), yes, just one more.
Telling me I should be saintly;
in my walk and talk and dress.
Sometimes what I really think is,
how does *he* know what is best?
Oh how I want to live just for me,
and do what e'er I want to do
but no . . . I'll just go on and suffer;
suffer for Jesus is what I do . . .
Suddenly the air is silent;
Not a sound disturbs the world!
And from Heaven's portalled hallways,
finally a sound is heard.

Booming as the crack of thunder,
yet as soft as misty rain;
powerful, yet oh so tender,
as a Mother's love toward pain.
In a rushing windy bower,
'tis a speaking voice I hear,
clear and soft, yet filled with power,
as it captivates my ear.

"How did you decide to suffer?
Who declared what you should do?
Do you know the suffering Savior?
Yes, please tell me, who told you?
You claim suffering is your burden,
yet I hear your wailing plea:
'I do without . . . I am suffering . . .
and I walk righteous . . .' Me, me, me.

"Don't you know you shame the glory,
of the suffering Christ?
When you puff and pine o'er burdens,
that you claim you have through life?
Have you given up the Heavens,
where your home once used to be?
Did you give your holy body
to be nailed upon a cruel tree?

"Were you spat upon and beaten?
Do they hate and mock your name?
Don't you know your claim to suffering,
also is your badge of shame?
But no, you do all in anger,
filled with pride and selfishness
claiming that you know the pathway
walked by Christ in humbleness.
Are you guiltless, pure and perfect?
Do you show them Christ in you?
Do you live your every second,
every hour . . . as Christ would do?

"No! You carry not His suffering,
'cause your pride must have its fill.
And you'll never walk as Christ did,
'til you walk Golgotha's hill.
Walk you must, in His own footsteps.
Walk you must, the road He trod.
His cross, you must lift and carry,
soaked in His own cleansing blood.
If you dare to turn from your pride,
and desire to be like Him,
you'll begin to walk as He did,
and yes . . . suffering will begin.

"Then you'll truly come to know Him,
and the pain within His heart,
for the lost . . . the beaten . . . broken . . .
and begin to know the part
of a suffering, serving saint,
living . . . loving . . . just like Christ,
'cause the joy of being like Him,
makes it worth what e'er the price,
to walk like the suffering Servant,
praying that the world will see
sacrifice, for their salvation,
while My Son, lives within thee."

Silence then . . . oh, dreaded silence,
brings conviction to my soul.
How could I have been so pious
acting such a shameful fool?
Seeing now with eyes wide open;
opened by God's chastening words,
hearing now what He has spoken,
in the thunder that I heard.

Selfishness escaped my bosom.
Pride just crumbled all around,
as my pious shame poured from me,
shedding tears upon the ground.

"Oh, dear Jesus, please forgive me,
for my weakness in the flesh,
bragging that I knew of suffering.
Fill me with Yourself, afresh.
Fill me, Lord, with Your own heart cry,
for the lost and dying world.
Close my mouth from ever speaking,
e'er again with prideful words.
Lord, I'll walk the road of suffering,
just to know Your will, divine,
even if that narrow way, Lord,
declares suffering must be mine.

And the loud noise of the lost ones,
will bring sorrow to my ear,
calling me to speak Your love Lord;
calling me to let them hear,
matchless love of Your own suffering,
there upon the Calvary tree,
suffering . . . bleeding . . . alone and dying,
forgiving them . . . forgiving me . . ."
Then a quiet came upon me,
as I looked into His face,
and He promised His strength to me
for defending His sweet grace.
Then He said, *"I'm sending you now,*
but know, when the suffering comes,
I'll not leave you, nor forsake you;
you are of My chosen ones."

Lord, please help me live with patience,
humbled by Your strengthening words,
as I pray that boasting and pride,
will ne'er again from me be heard.
Help me walk like Him, my Savior,
who suffered for my sin and shame.
The crucified heart of my dear Christ,
quietly, humbly, may I gain.
May I seek the joy before me,
even though it bears a price,
that I'll know the joy of suffering . . .
suffering for my precious Christ.

LIVING BY FAITH

❧ ❧ ❧

When Jesus called Lazarus
to come out from the tomb,
a walking dead man wrapped in cloth
is what we got to see.
But the grave clothes could not hold Him,
they had to turn Him loose,
while the people cried in amazement,
"Lord, is this true? Can this thing be?"

The storm was such a tempest
in a raging darkened night,
but Jesus? He was sleeping,
just as peaceful as could be.
While disciples in confusion,
wrought with fear, and awful fright
cried out, "Master, wake up, help us.
Master help us! What about me?"

What about me, Lord?
What about me?
I know that by faith in God
you walked upon the sea.
And by faith you spoke, and legions
of demons had to flee,
but what about me, Lord?
What about Me?

Jesus prayed in faith and gave
many thousands, food to eat,
and in Gethsemane's Garden,
by faith He made a humble plea.
Then on Calvary, He cried, "Forgiven!"
and it set the captives free.
But, what about me, Lord?
What about me?
What about me, Lord,
what about me?

Yes, you left Your home in Heaven
to come here and make your plea,
that if we put our faith in You
we can live eternally.

I know many words and books are written
'bout Him hanging on the tree,
so now I have to wonder,
What about me, Lord?
What about me?

Jesus walked upon the water.
I'm as sure as sure can be.
And yes He even gave His life
that day at Calvary.

So won't you let this question
search your heart along with me:
Can I truly be like other folks
who live by faith for all can see?

Dare I ask,
What about me, Lord?
What about me?

WHY REPENT?

I'll Leave It Up to You

❧ ❧ ❧

Momma told me not to play
with fire . . . I might get burned,
yet in her wisdom she always said,
"I'll leave it up to you."

The law was drafted for our good
by wise men full of honor,
but that can't force you to obey.
They leave it up to you.

Yes, evil lurks around the bend
and at each corner's turn,
when darkness comes to hide the light
from yonder sky of blue,

where the lion lurks within the grass
to kill unwitting prey,
but that prey could stay the lions mouth
if prey knew what to do.

So "why repent" when sin is fun
and Hell's not yet half full?
Because you'd please the Lord my God.
Is that the thing to do?

God didn't leave you all alone,
to be a victim or fall prey,
to Satan's wiles and tempting ploys
by which he'd capture you.

God sent His Son to be the Light
and save you from the dark
that hides within the corners of
your soul's deep mires and moods.

He does not force you to accept
His sacrificial Lamb.
He leaves the choices to be made
by none other than you.

No, He won't force you to repent
and have your sins forgiven.
He will not force you to receive . . .
He leaves it up to you.

So now it's yours to wrestle with.
'Tis you who makes the choice.
You have the freedom to decide,
so it must be *your voice.*

But rest assured God does not sleep.
He patiently awaits
to hear you ask if you can enter
through those heavenly gates.

So while yet Heaven waits above,
or Hell below, eternally . . .
Satan says,
"No, don't repent!"
God's speaks and says,
"It's up to you."

TOO LATE TO HARVEST

❧ ❧ ❧

I know the Word of God has said
that I should plant some seed.
And surely to God's written Word,
you know I should give heed.
It speaks of rich, or rocky soil,
or somewhere in between.
So, what I want to find is some
that's pure and fresh and clean.

I'll go next door and see the man
that's always on the go.
Yet never does he go to church,
at least not that I know.

Oh, what a rough old man he is;
he drinks and smokes and swears.
He's eaten up with selfishness
and other worldly cares.
His fingernails are dirty
and filled with grease and oil.
I know that he must be the one
that's called the rocky soil.

I think I'll pass him up today
and look for someone else;
someone more refined and clean;
someone more like myself.
Yeah, I'll go on as duty bound
and find a piece of land
where I can plant this precious seed,
with my own loving hand.

I know the hospital is near
so I'll go visit there.
Perhaps I'll find a nice old patient,
who has clean hands and hair.

So upwards on the winding path
you find your traveling goes,
expecting you will find the place
to plant as you suppose.
You stand before the doors black number
staring from its face,
and you inhale the mixture of
the odors in this place.
The alcohol for rubbing wrinkled,
old, and dying skin,
and medicines to care for sickness
lingering deep within.
Your stomach says, "Get me away
from all this putridness."
And as you walk away you're pleased,
you really must confess.
Because you know without a doubt
this cannot be the ground
where God expects to plant this precious
seed you carry 'round.

Oh well, it's just another day,
so I'll search on some more,
to find that perfect, clean, rich soil
that I am looking for.
I know that God will show me where to
plant this seed today,
because I said, "God's written word,
I surely would obey."
So I'll just walk a little while
into that part of town,
where someone of my class and breeding
isn't commonly found.
I know that I'll impress them with
the ways that I possess
and surely just to be like me,
their sins they will confess.
Then I'll plant seed within their heart
and surely reap reward,
for doing all that I have done
while working for the Lord.

Oh! There's a beggar sitting there;
surely I can plant some seed,
because he will rejoice that I
came here to give him what he needs.

"Let go of me you dirty tramp!
What do you think you're doing?
You touch my clothing just once more
and you'll find I'll be suing
you, for having my clothes cleaned . . ."
Oh . . . you're so rough and so unshorn.
You must be as the Bible says:
the ground that's full of thorns.

It's not to you I'll sow this precious
seed from my dear hands.
I'd sooner cast them far upon
the dry and tepid desert sands.
You'd only choke and strangle it,
as soon as it would bloom.
I'll find a suitable land for it,
and leave this place of gloom.

So on and on the wandering goes,
and ne'er do you find soil to please.
So now you sit and rest awhile
enjoying your sweet life of ease.

What is that sound?
It seems like trumpets blowing in the east.
My goodness, it's the Clarion call,
"Come to the Master's feast!"
"I'm here," I said. "It's me oh, Lord;
I'm ready for my crown!"
And as I stood my eyes went to
the seeds I dropped upon the ground.

Too late! It is too late to plant;
it's too late to have a harvest,
because my selfish pride has said,
"I'm better than the rest."

Where God directed I refused
to place seeds in the ground,
and now in broken, selfish shame
with empty hands I'm found.
I walked away from what I thought
was soil all full of thorns.
I passed the man with such poor manners
in clothing tattered and torn.
I saw my neighbor only as
a man with dirty skin.
If I'd but had a spiritual eye
I might have seen within.
Then I'd have seen the hearts,
that God had readied for the seed
but in my selfish foolishness
I bowed to prideful needs.
And now I see the rocks and thorns
which I thought I should flee,
were living within my own heart.
That's all that I was seeing.

If all we ever see is rocks,
while searching for the goal
we'll never get to plant the seeds
within the fertile soil.
Don't say, "I will," and then put off
'til you feel more inclined.
Before you hardly blink your eye,
it will be harvest time.
At harvest time you'll have no crown
to lay at Jesus' feet.
And you will have no fruit to bring
into the marriage feast.
So don't delay, plant seed, plant seed.
Plant seed without delay.
And bring the lives that you have won,
to lay at Jesus' feet.

Plant seed today for harvest time.
Plant seed – some souls to win.
And know the joy of seeing God
as He reaps your harvest in.

WHAT ABOUT ME

❧ ❧ ❧

In the mountains, in the valleys,
in the woodlands, by the sea
youngsters search the age-old question:
"Who am I supposed to be?"
There's Confucius and Galileo,
old Mark Twain, and Washington:
Millions mark the history pages:
Who shall I be like? Which one?

On the street cars men are sitting,
while old ladies stand alone.
What is proper? What is kindness?
What I see and hear at home?
Or is decency a mystery
that has faded into time?
Is it just my wistful dreaming;
some old dreams passed on by time?

Preacher tells me,
"Love thy neighbor,
it's the word from God above."
Yet at home what I am seeing
surely ain't that kind of love.
There has got to be an answer;
one that I can hold on to.
Should I be like this or that one?
Mom, or Dad, or him, or you?

Yes, I'm trying hard to grow up
so I'll know just who to be.
What example should I look to?
Who am I? Who should I be?

Please, don't think I'm being silly;
I'm just searching in my youth.
Don't give up and turn away now
with an ugly, "What's the use?"

So adult please listen closely
when you're questioned by a child.
You are looking at a struggle
that is serious . . . not mild.

You think, "Why should I help children
find their way through this old world,
when so many stand in anger,
glaring, with a lip up-curled."
Seeming so rebellious, angry;
looking like they just don't care.
Have you ever thought,
"Who showed them?
Who carved the way that led them here?"

Dad's so perfect . . . but he cusses;
Mom's so pure . . . but she still drinks.
In the meantime there's nobody
that will hear what I might think.

"What about your hair," they holler.
"What about your room? . . . A mess!
And your friends just drive me crazy
with the stupid way they dress."
"They're so dumb," is what you say
or, "They couldn't hold a thought!"
If that's true, then what they are,
is just the way that we've been taught.

Yes, I could become a lawyer
or an addict on the street,
one day lying in the gutter
looking for a bite to eat.
But we're looking for examples;
someone who will show the way;
someone who is really living
all the things I hear them say.

I'm just trying hard to grow up;
I need to know who I should be,
but if I live what I am seeing . . .
how can I live *perfectly?*

Should I really try to live up
to examples that I see
when I don't think that you really care
what is happening within me.

Truth is, yes, I'd rather give up,
than to think that I should be
all the terrible examples
that your life is showing me.

Should I trust in Galileo?
Preacher, do you preach what's true?
Do I search the history pages?
Mom, or Dad . . . could it be you?

I just want to live and grow up,
into all that I can be.
Gee, I wish I could find someone
who would help *me* to find me.

Will you mark their history pages
with a cheer of, "Yes. Well done!"
Or is that a dream that's faded?
You must make the choice: which one?

They have mountains, they have valleys,
they have stormy troubled seas.
Youngsters search in you for answers.
Are you
what you're supposed to be?

THE MOST BEAUTIFUL BIBLE

❧ ❧ ❧

As I sat there with my head in my hands
I don't think there's anyone that understands.
The radio is blaring all those words
it's really stupid stuff,
let me tell you what I heard:
There's a guy like a carnival man,
hawkin' his wares.
The way he's going about it
sure wouldn't make me care.
Inside it just leaves me feeling all numb.
I guess he's religious alright
but boy, it just sounds dumb . . .
when I hear this kind of junk.

"Come one, come all,
come big and small;
the deal of a lifetime is here.
Come young and old, come everyone;
this offer may soon disappear.
Withe edges of gold and letters so bold.
Come read the greatest story ever told!
You can get it in blue and burgundy too.
We'll even put your name on it for you.
Come, hurry now! Man alive,
this amazing Bible is only
nine-ninety-five!"

Then I looked down beneath my palm
at the pages all tattered and torn
and said, "Don't kid me. I can plainly see
the most beautiful Bible is well worn."

How many people have passed this way
and opened these pages and heard
God speak to them in a special way
from this, His sweet holy Word.

I JUST DON'T FEEL LIKE GOING TO HEAVEN

❧ ❧ ❧

I visited John the other day,
and he said he didn't feel good.
"I'm awfully tired," is all that he'd say;
He just didn't feel like he should.

He said to me,"It's the flu you know,
and I guess I could really die."
I said, "John, let me just have a look,"
and I peered into his eyes.

"John, why do you think that you're so sick
that death could be the end?"
He said, "Well, I just *feel* that way . . .
all over, from end to end."

I went to see John the other day,
and John didn't look so good.
There he lay within the casket;
dead as a piece of wood.

It wasn't the flu that took his life;
he just had a simple cold.
But nine months later, lying in his bed,
John quietly died from being old.

When John *felt* that he had the flu,
a doctor he would not see.
He also *felt* he'd go to Heaven,
but that . . . not positively.

I asked him why he *felt* he'd go
to Heaven when he would die.
He said, "Well I *feel* like I am not so bad;
I'm really a pretty nice guy."

I told him, "John, if it's just *feelings,*
then that's all you're going to get.
It's really not enough, John.
There's much more than just *feeling* it!"

I said, "John, you remember the flu . . .
When you *felt* you were so ill?"
He said, "Yeah I know,
I was well the next day,
and I didn't even take a pill."

"You see John, you didn't have the flu
but just had *feelings*, right?
So John, the *feelings* didn't get you.
The *feelings* didn't take your life."

"So I'll tell you something, dear John,
that you *sincerely* need to know.
Just *feeling* you'll make it to Heaven
doesn't mean you'll get to go."

"It takes much more than cozy *feelings*
to really become saved.
You can *feel* that you know Jesus,
and to sin still be a slave."

"Would you like to really know, John,
and *be sure* that Heaven is yours?
And when you see the river, Jordan,
you'll make it to the safer shore?"

"John, will you let Jesus save you . . .
make your heart clean, white, and pure?
Then you won't *feel* like you're going to Heaven;
instead you'll be really sure."

Well, John accepted Jesus that day
and took Christ into his heart.
John said he wanted full assurance,
with all feelings set apart.

I don't want to just have *feelings.*
I know there's more than that to get.
I *really* want to know for sure;
I want more than *feeling* it.

So I looked at John's old empty body
laying cold, there in the box.
"You know you lost him Satan,
you treacherous lying fox!"

"I know you told John many times,
'Don't bother with religious stuff.
As long as you can *feel good* about it,
well, John, that's good enough'."

But John got his full assurance.
He nailed it down good and tight.
He accepted forgiveness from Jesus.
Yes, John got saved alright.

So I join with John in saying this:
while I'm on this earthly tour,
"I don't just *feel* like going to Heaven;
I've made *absolutely sure*."

What about you my lonely friend?
What has Satan said to you?

Has he told you that
just feeling you'll make it
is all you need to do?

THE LION AND THE RABBIT

❧ ❧ ❧

A lion met a tiger
as they drank beside the pool.
Said the tiger to the lion,
"Why do you roar
like such a fool?"

"That's not foolish,"
said the lion,
with a twinkle in his eyes.
"They all call me
the King of beasts,
because I advertise!"

A rabbit heard them talking,
And ran home like a streak.
He thought he'd try the lion's plan,
but his roar was just as squeak.

A fox who heard the rabbit,
had his dinner in the woods . . .

**So when you advertise, my friends,
be sure you've got the goods!**

LORD, WHAT WOULD YOU HAVE ME TO DO?

❧ ❧ ❧

I'm a man of unclean lips
and I dwell in a world of the same.
I do what I'm not supposed to do,
and Lord, I feel ashamed.
I don't believe You could use me Lord,
because I've been so bad,
but Lord if You'll just touch me once,
I'll give You all that I have.

What would You have me to do Lord;
what would You have me to be?
Isn't there someplace in Your fields?
Someplace to use even me?
I'm filled with *self,* and I'm incomplete,
and that is why I cry.
Please make me clean and use me Lord;
use me before I die.

I'm not what is called handsome
and my speech is poor as can be,
but I'm sick of feeling empty, dear Lord.
Can You find a place for me?
What would You have me to do Lord?
What would You have me to be?
Isn't there someplace in Your fields?
Someplace to use even me?

The apostle Paul was a little man;
just barely five feet tall.
He brought death and destruction
everywhere he went.
Yes, Paul had done it all.
Though Peter denied that he knew You, Lord,
as his Lord and as his friend,
yet he said three times that he loved You Lord,
and You used him in the end.

What would You have me to do Lord?
What would You have me to be?
Isn't there someplace in Your fields?
Someplace to use even me?
Peter had to hear the rooster crow,
and Paul had to be struck blind.
While I sit here in the darkness, Lord,
don't you have something in mind?

Take me not to be great, or mighty;
famous is not what I'm asking to be.
I just want You to use me Lord;
whatever You ask of me.
Yes Lord, I yield to Your full control,
to do with me as You please.
I just want the joy of serving You,
with my heart at last in peace.

Lord cleanse from me my unclean lips
that bring upon You shame.
And take my heart and head too;
Lord cleanse them all the same.
Come live within me, Holy Spirit,
and fill me with Your love, divine.
I want my life to be fully used;
hereafter Yours, no longer mine.

No matter how small the task may be,
I'll do as You tell me to do.
I just need to be Your servant Lord,
doing some service for You.
Use me where You want me Lord;
wherever You want me to be.
I know there must be a place in Your fields;
a place to use even me.

WHAT A REVELATION

❧ ❧ ❧

Oh, book of Revelation; what mysteries you hold.
"One cannot understand it," so often I've been told.
The many headed creatures, the hail, and fiery storms,
"Don't try to understand it," so often I've been warned.

"It deals in rhymes and riddles," is often said to me.
"The book of Revelation? 'Tis best just let it be."

But in my inner spirit, a restlessness prevails,
to know about the fire, the creatures, and the hail.

The name says Revelation:
To me that means "reveal."
So why should I believe that
it is locked and tightly sealed?
Wouldn't it just be a waste
of God's own precious Word,
to keep His secrets from mankind;
to ne'er again be heard?

So what about the Dragon,
and the woman with the Child?
To think they might mean something real,
yeah, does seem pretty wild.
There are so many angels there,
just flying all around.
Some pour strange stuff into the air
and some upon the ground.

What about the three and half times?
The times and time again?
What about the earthquakes, and blood . . .
And, yes . . . what about Sin?

My friend, don't get all tied up
by worrying about this book.
It's time to clear your thinking.
Time for a second look.

The book is Revelation;
it tells what God has shown
to us from in His heavenly place
where He's seated on His throne.

Yes, there is symbolism there,
mysterious and deep.
But there's also a serious thought,
and this you need to keep:

The end-times aren't so scary,
for those who know the Lord.
They know that you can be kept safe,
by His own living Word.

And there's a matter of much importance,
that you should understand.
You need to be about winning souls,
and leading them to His hand.

The book of Revelation is meant
to be a warning cry,
to win the lost at any cost;
to find them now before they die.

The plagues, the vials, the fire,
all tell of things to come,
that God will do upon this earth,
just days before He comes.

He'll wipe away forever more
the choices He gave to man.
At that time all decisions made,
will be at His own hand.

The one that's lost will still be lost,
for all eternity.
Unless they come to Christ in time . . .
brought there by you or me.

So put away the worrying,
'bout number six, six, six.
Don't listen to what Satan says,
believing in his tricks.

Let's lead the lost to Jesus Christ
while there's still time on earth.
Let's take them all to Him, the Savior;
the One who gives re-birth.

Mysteries, rhymes and riddles
are all meant to be heard.
Everything from Genesis on
is still God's perfect Word.

Take it in, and eat it up;
live it, sleep it, night and day.
God surely will reveal to you
what the Revelations say.

There is no need to be afraid
of what's written in God's Word.
Go ask Him like you'd ask your daddy.
Yes, you will be heard.

Thunder and lighting from the sky
and vials being poured out.
Anguish, screaming, and crying is heard,
and many a heart-rending shout.

Yes, those will be some awful times
for those who have earned such pain.
But what you'll see and hear that's dreadful,
won't be for the *born-again.*

There is no need to fear them,
these words of inspiration.
They come from the heart
of my heavenly Father,
who will keep you
through Revelations.

THERE'S A BREACH IN THE WALL

❧ ❧ ❧

"There's a breach in the wall,"
calls the captain of the guard.
"Who's watching the field?
Who's watching the yard?"
When the enemy came
all was silent and still,
so he breached the wall
at the top of the hill.

We had just joined forces
and our strength was renewed.
We had formed into ranks;
we had passed in review.
We'd inspected the armor
and all felt prepared,
but we didn't hear the laughter
in the enemy's lair.

We were self-satisfied
that our weapons were clean.
And just to be sure,
we rechecked everything.
But lying in wait
at the foot of our pride,
was the place he had chosen
for his soldiers to hide.

We had climbed up the mountain;
we thought that we knew
the essential things
that we had to do
to keep the strong enemy
out of the camp,
but we found that our best
was a feeble attempt.

We had bullets of prayer;
our shields were called praise.
So we lay down to rest
at the end of our day.
But the watchman we set
was still suffering from pride,
and he went to the guard
being self-satisfied.
He was all puffed up with,
"I've done things so well!"
Yet he'd not locked the gate
to the keeper of Hell.
And while in the night watch,
the guard was asleep,
the enemy was ready
and he made his great leap.

"Over the field wall,
See . . . here they come!"
But we'd laid down our shields.
We could not find our guns!
Where is the praise
we had used for our strength?
"Look there. He's coming up over the fence!"

Our weapons were lying
about in the dust,
forgotten and dirty,
now damaged by lust.
Our pride was the culprit
that set us at ease
as we thought we could do
whatever we pleased.

We had paid up and prayed up
and made up our minds
that we were so safe
on the enemy lines,
that we could take ease
and sleep just one night
After all, his was *wrong,*
and our side is *right!*

And then as we slept
in our sweet piety,
in a moment of shame
came the sly enemy.
He tore down our fences
and breached our great wall,
and the shame of our pride
was the cause of it all.

What a lesson was coming . . .
Our pride had to fall.
Yes, the enemy had breached
our self-righteous wall.

Through our sin and our pride
the enemy came
and the fall of our camp
was a terrible shame.
Our hearts were weeping just inside the gate
as the enemy shot us with self-doubt and hate.
'Neath our fences of sin
and our walls of great pride,
the enemy had found
a good place to hide.

Do you think you've arrived.
Do you think you've attained?
Then hear this, "It's your loss
and the enemy's gain."
Cry out to your captain
to keep you on guard,
because losing the battle
is shamefully hard.

You've been trusted with faith:
a dependable shield,
to protect you from harm
out there in the field,
and a spiritual sword
that the enemy hates
'cause it cuts thru temptation
and destroys Hell's gates.

You've been trusted with truth;
your loins wrapped about,
and its power is awesome
when you give it a shout.
With righteousness firmly
attached to your chest
you'll defeat all his men
from the least to the best.

But the peace of the Gospel
we often mistake
as a time made for resting,
so a small nap we take,
'tho the peace of the Gospel
that is built in our shoes
is to give strength for standing
not for taking a snooze.

With a salvation helmet
sitting firm on our head
we are dressed out as soldiers,
but we're sleepers instead.
When the enemy comes,
we're to win over him
instead of just resting
in greed, lust, and sin.

Yet with all we're given,
how often we fall
to the strength of the enemy
as he breaches the wall.
So take heed fellow warrior:
strip off sin and pride.
Don't allow those dark places
where the enemy can hide.

"Call out the Captain in charge of the guard.
Watch close o'er the field and the fence and the yard!"
Let our Captain, the Lord, lead us on to the fight
and be a good watchman, both day and night."

With Him as the leader
in charge over all
the enemy, Satan,
can ne'er breach the wall.
But if you begin resting
whenever you feel
and you put up your sword,
or lay aside your shield,
you may think he's not paying
attention to you,
and that's exactly the thought
he's been wanting from you.
When you've turned aside praying
and the strength of your faith,
the enemy comes boldly,
right through the front gate.

And if you set a watch
but the watchman is weak,
a crack in your wall
of defense he will seek.
Then up o'er the wall
with his forces he'll swarm
But remember . . .
JESUS can conquer the storm!

Rely on your armor
with faith as your shield.
Then to Satan's fiery darts
you never will yield.
Make God your strong watchman
to guard over your walls,
and to Satan's temptations
He will not let you fall.
Open your heart
and your will to God's reach.
And your walls of protection
will never be breached.
Turn the battle on Satan
and his armies will fail,
for against God's Word,
Hell's gates cannot prevail.

Be a soldier . . .
aware of lust, shame, and pride,
so that Satan's forces
will have nowhere to hide.
Chink your walls with God's mortar
formed by His holy Word.
Let the battle cry, "JESUS!"
loud and clearly be heard.

With the light of His Gospel
shining forth day and night,
take the battle to Satan;
put his thousands to flight.

Then the vict'ry of salvation
will all the world reach,
and you'll ne'er hear the cry;
"The walls have been breached!"

THE MAKING OF A MAN

❧ ❧ ❧

I cannot count the Sundays
that I have been to church . . .
The offering plate comes to me
and I give . . . (but not if it hurts).
I'm satisfied with my own life;
I have no sense of loss.
But the way the preacher preaches . . .
I wonder . . . have I counted the cost?
I don't see Jesus as he does.
I just don't know what to say . . .
I wonder what is in me,
that keeps me from being that way?
He speaks of joy in obedience,
and laying my life down,
to win one day in glory,
to place at His feet . . . a crown.
I feel there's something I'm missing,
but I want it to be mine,
if I'm to know the joys of Heaven,
and languish in His presence sublime.

Oh God, I want to know You
and what You want me to be,
even if the price You require
is to give my all to Thee.
Burn out my self-sufficiency.
Burn out my pride and it's shame,
and set my life afire
by the fuel of Jesus' name.

Oh God, consume my being.
Make me the work of Your hand.
Destroy the *will* within me,
to believe in the *self-made* man.
Cover me with ashes
to remember evermore,
that sufficient I will never be,
without You, Jesus, as my source.

A HIGHWAY CALLED HOLINESS

❧ ❧ ❧

We come to him, the Crucified,
to have our sins forgiven.
We trust and we accept His Word,
and know we're bound for Heaven.

We breath, we live, we laugh, we sing,
we want to please the Lord.
And we believe we're doing all
we can to live His Word.

But underneath we feel the tug
of when the flesh was king,
and yet sometimes we realize
we're lacking that *something*.

Our thoughts sometimes will stray too far
from what we know is right.
And guilt will find us often times,
to bring us sleepless nights.

I went to church just yesterday,
and I've read my Bible through,
but deep within, my Spirit said,
"There's still more left to do."

I struggle in my finite mind,
to find the right pathway,
because I know there's something calling,
quiet and far away.

It is a pathway I must take,
where other saints have trod.
It is the pathway that was made,
by the Holy Son of God.

A trail of tears, I may will find,
if I would walk that path,
and yet I know that there are many,
other ones who have.

I have not seen the feet of Him
who walked in lowliness,
but there upon His face is etched,
Highway of Holiness.

It's such a private walk to make,
though yet, not all alone.
behind the veil we know He waits;
the One whose blood atones.

The One from manger to the Cross,
Walked pure . . . and without sin.
The Christ of love, the Christ of joy,
the Christ of peace within.

The Christ that walks within a heart
which yields itself to God.
The Christ that takes us to the path,
that only saints can trod.

Unseen by man with naked eye,
void yet of Godly gain,
there is a place we step across,
that reads, "Now Christ will reign."

Across the line we step by choice,
in quiet peacefulness,
with full assurance that we step,
into Christ's Holiness.

WILL A MAN ROB GOD?

❧ ❧ ❧

Me, rob a man? Me rob a man?
Oh dear sir, goodness no!
Why would you ask me such a question
that is sharpened so?
You point it as a dagger,
to cut my very heart.
In such a shameful sort of thing,
no, I would never take a part!

I am a man of honor;
of highest integrity.
What makes you bring this question sir,
to someone such as me?
I pay my way most honestly
in everything I do.
Perhaps t'would be more fitting
if I'd ask the same of you?

Oh? 'tisn't money that the searching
is clearly bringing out?
It's something deeper? Larger?
Whatever do you talk about?

Lurking in the shadows,
I know this man must be
seeking for my hidden man,
and He won't let me be,
until He finds the secrets
of my life I've hidden there,
that aren't His for the knowing of,
if I don't want to share.

I have a right to live my life
and be just who I am,
without this one from Galilee
revealing every plan.

I beg your pardon, sir. Your question?
Did you speak again?
You ask me things with riddles
which aren't very plain.

How many hours do I have
from sun to rising sun?
Why, but of course I have the same
as every other one.

And what days do I own sir?
How many did I make?
Oh come you cannot be sincere, my man.
Come now, for goodness sake.

Create an hour all by myself?
Man, you don't know what you ask.
No human being is able
to accomplish such a task.

The days belong to God, dear sir;
the weeks, the months, the years.
'Tis quite a foolish question
that you ask of me, I fear.

What do you mean,
"If they are God's,
why do I use them all?"
I have a right to use them, sir,
spring, summer, winter, fall."

Again you call me robber?
And you say that I rob God?
I give my tithe, attend the church,
and I never yawn or nod.

I also pay attention;
I pay attention well,
and know that I obey the Word
or face eternal Hell.

So, sir how dare you? Yes, indeed!
Suppose you make it clear
exactly what I'm guilty of;
oh, I can't wait to hear.

You say I'm lacking honesty
by all that you have seen?
And I must yield before the Lord
to become honest, guiltless, clean?

Does God allow me money,
that I may give some back?
Why but of course, and honestly,
I'm always keeping track.

Does God supply my health, you say?
Does He yet give me life?
Does He not give me strength and breath?
Correct, sir! . . . Right each time.

So how much do I work for him?
How much do I give back?
How can I give him what is gone,
forever to the past?
Give time to God? Man are you daft?
To work for God? I say . . .
God doesn't need for me to work;
He does things all HIS way.

Do what? You say this is His way
of doing things on earth?
And He needs me to win the lost
so He can bring re-birth?
And He can't do it without me?
He says that I must see
that I'm robbing Him if I don't give,
and there'll be penalties?

I'll lose rewards, and I'll lose joy?
I'll lose my peace within?
'Cause robbing God at any point
will still be counted sin?

Would I rob God and be a thief?
Would I refuse my call?
No thank you kindly sir, I think,
I should be giving all.

Who are you sir, to know these things;
how did you know of me?
You are the One who created time,
since all eternity.
Dear sir . . . Oh Jesus, dear . . .
the Savior of my soul.
The eyes of my poor spirit see;
yes Lord, 'tis You I owe.

My tithe, my praise, my love, and time,
I owe all to you
Forgive my ignorance, loving God,
from now on I will do
this one more thing that I may just
a little higher soar,
and be in You Lord, more complete
than e'er I was before.

I'll go to work, I’ll give, I'll labor;
my time will be Your own.
I'll sow the Gospel seeds of love,
that I have never sown.
A *robber* Lord I shall not be
because I owe my all to You
So, help me Lord,
please give me strength
to do all I should do.

THE INDWELLING POWER

❧ ❧ ❧

Walking in sorrow and sadness.
Living in suffering and shame
Thinking that life is just hopeless;
never to be free from my pain.
God has sent Jesus to save you
and you have invited Him in.
Then why does your spirit continue
walking and living in sin?

Oh man of the Earth can't you see it?
Your flesh is always in charge.
Why do you give *me such* a small place
and your flesh a place that's so large?
Your flesh loves the sin of the worldly
for *self* cannot be satisfied.
It stains you with shame for your actions
which you are not able to hide.

It devours and demands even more sin,
the larger it grows in your breast,
because there's no power to stop it
and you never will have time to rest.
The fighting, the struggling, the losing,
don't you ever get tired of it all?
While you're trying to walk, you're stumbling.
When you try to run you just fall.

And the failures that keep you distracted?
They're part of the enemy's plan.
He wants you to bow to his spirit
in defeat just as long as he can.
But you know you belong to the Father.
He's the Victor of spiritual war.
It's not only the bread that you live by.
God has given you so much more.

If you lay down the baggage you carry
of self, sin, and pride, and lust,
then the Spirit of God can come fill you
and give you the power to trust.

You can trust Him to fight all your battles.
You can trust Him to be your best friend.
You can trust Him to keep you from falling.
He will fight for you right to the end.

No it won't be the end of the battles,
you will probably fight evermore.
But with God's Holy Spirit within you,
you have already won the war.

The choice is yours now dear pilgrim.
You can walk in the strength of your flesh,
or be filled with God's Holy Spirit,
with a power divine, full and fresh.

The suffering from shame will be over.
With His Spirit you will be one.
So why don't you turn to the Father?
and say,
"Holy Spirit, now come.
The self-man I no longer treasure.
He'll be my master no more.
I yield to the power of Your Spirit.
Come fill me with Yourself evermore."

CELEBRATE

It's Not Time to Celebrate

❧ ❧ ❧

The religious men had gotten their way.
This Jewish Teacher was going to pay.
He claims that He is God's only Son.
Let's crucify Him with the other ones!

"Hey, they're taking three out to the skull.
They're crucifying on the third hour.
That's nine o'clock; let's not be late.
Let's go with them and celebrate."

They dropped the cross into the ground,
with a horrible thudding sound.
The spikes were driven one, two, three,
and Jesus was nailed to the tree.

"Break out the dice; let's play a game
for the robe of the Son of Man.
Let Him come down if He's really God;
let Him come down . . . if He can."

They gave Him vinegar mingled with gall,
but He said, "It's finished." That was all.
So the three sat down to watch Him there.
It was party time so they didn't care.

They gambled, they laughed,
they called Him names
while saying,
"This Jesus is really *insane!*
How can He then the temple raise,
after being in the grave three days?"

"Just read the sign up over His head:
'The King of the Jews' it says.
Yeah I know that's what they wrote
but, the King of the Jews is dead."

Then the veil of the temple
was torn in two.
And they asked each other,
"What should we do?
I thought that this was party time,
but it's gotten dark
and there's no sunshine.
Come on, let's run man.
Don't hesitate.
Let's save ourselves if it's not too late!"

But one lone soldier stood at the cross.
looking at Jesus, thinking,
"What a loss . . .
I drove the nails,
and I drove them hard,
into the hands of the Son of God."

"I believe my hammer started a war,
that's going to continue evermore,
and surely the world will pay for its sin
until the *real* celebration begins."

"Son of God, if You'll let me come,
I'd like to ask, if it's not too late.
Will You take me to Your heavenly home,
to be with You when You celebrate?"

"I know that it's too early now,
but I'll give You my blood, tears and sweat
and until then I'll plant and I'll plow
'cause, it's not time to celebrate yet."

ON THE ROAD AGAIN

❧ ❧ ❧

"On the road again . . ."
was a phrase I used to say,
singing at a swanky club or in a cheap café.
Did it really matter where
I'd sing, or sleep, or go?
No, not really, 'cause I didn't care
that my *worth* was very, very low.

"Who I am," was plastic.
A "make believe", no doubt,
'cause, "You are just nobody,"
was what the devil would shout.

But oh, the road grew weary
and the way was always dark.
And it didn't really matter
'cause I had a *loser's* heart.
So the devil had his say so
and my life was ruled by him.
He'd kick me out and holler,
"You! Git goin'. Hit the road again!"

He would say that I was worthless
and I'd buy it every time,
'til the day that I saw Jesus
standing on that road of mine.
With a glow of love around Him;
He held both arms out to me.
"Come to Me. Be My child.
You are valuable to Me."

Now He reassures me daily
that I'm worthwhile to Him.
And the road I walk is holy,
because Jesus lives within.

LORD, USE ME TO MINISTER

❧ ❧ ❧

Lord, what am I to do today?
I'm just so covered up.
I've got to get my neighbor straight
and lots of other stuff.
The world is in an awful mess.
It's falling all apart.
I just don't understand mankind.
Oh, he has such a wicked heart.

And You God . . . You want me to use
my time to find a mirror?
What was it that You said to me?
"In there, I'll see an error."
But, Lord, don't You remember me?
Don't You know who I am?
I'm *born-again* and go to church.
I've been *saved* since I was ten.

But Lord . . . is that one really me?
The image in the glass?
I thought that I was spiritual.
A regular *coup de grace*.
But the image says I'll need to die
before I'll ever see
the thrill of working in Your fields . . .
Your fields of ministry.

Then change me Lord, and teach me how
You want my life to be,
that I may serve from this day on
in Christian Ministry.
Give me the thrill of knowing, Lord,
that I have had a hand
in seeing others find their way
into Your *promised land.*

NO COMPROMISE

❧ ❧ ❧

I walked a road of safety,
cleansed and fully committed to God.
And nothing there could touch me
as I'd see Him smile and nod.
I committed all my ways to Him,
and He was committed to me.
But then I went out on my own,
'til His face I could not see.

The years grew so much longer
and my commitment vanished away.
I compromised everything to the world;
more and more with each passing day.
Soon my life in the Savior was empty.
I'd used it for the lure of my sin.
But in my heart a voice still said
I'd not be left or forsaken by Him.

My sins grew so much stronger
that they broke my body in pain
and ruined my pride in Jesus
'til it filled me with my shame.
To be like Jesus, showing forth His love
was something I could no longer claim.
It hurt me to know that I'd failed Him
and tarnished His wonderful name.

I longed for the days when my Savior
walked with me in fellowship sweet.
I wanted Him back in my life;
to be His and be made complete.
So back to the alter of mercy
to the humble beginnings I knew,
I went with a broken heart
seeking His forgiveness anew.

I cried at the altar of Mercy,
"Change my heart, oh God, once more.
Purge me with some of your hyssop;
and forgive me, oh Lord, in full.
Renew within me Your spirit;
wash me clean and pure by your love.
Take my yielded heart and mend it,
by Your precious power from above."

My will is to walk the road again,
that goes the way the You've gone.
It doesn't matter where I've been
or where my erring steps have trod.
The only thing that matters now
is being where You are,
and knowing that forever more
I'm safe in the arms of God.

IN HIS PRESENCE, PEACE BE STILL

❧ ❧ ❧

Out upon the near horizon
brews another stormy day.
Swirling dark depression,
once again will come my way.
Clouds with threats of sadness,
rolling o'er the sky,
while my tired heart is asking,
"Why Lord? Why?"

Pitifully again I go
into my dungeons dark and deep,
dragging up the memories
of old past fears and grief,
where my aching body cries
for all the pain it bears,
and the Tempter calls out tauntingly,
"You know that no one cares!"

"Who are you to have the peace
and love that others know?
Why should you have joy upon
your face like others show?
When have you done anything
to soften all their pain?"
Constantly accusing me
time and time again.

On and on with deepening sadness,
those messages ebb and flow.
Wrapping my mind in it's grasp
never to let go.
Like the angry, ripping, tide,
from a boisterous sea,
swirling troubled thoughts pile high,
and beat me to my knees.

"Oh, God, why must it be this way?
When do I find rest?
When do I find peace and comfort,
for this aching breast?"

Then within the thunder clouds
a tiny light appears,
to grow and gleam and glisten,
as I watch it, drawing near.

Faintly then I see a figure,
walking deep within the glow,
silencing my beating heart,
because somehow I know . . .
that there amid the crashing thunder,
and the angry raging sky,
is the peace that I have dreamed of,
within my troubled mind.

The figure draws still nearer,
through my puzzled, blurry sight,
as He turns my yawning darkness,
into a morning light.

My vision becomes clearer
and I can see that it is He!
The One who calms the winds and storms;
the Man from Galilee.

And all around me peace and love,
is all that I can feel,
as He quietly walks upon my storm,
and whispers, "Peace be still."

Why do I let sorrow
from this angry world withhold
all the precious treasures,
that He offers for my soul,
robbing me of joy and peace
He wants to bring to me?
Because I simply see what is,
instead of what could be.

WHAT HAVE I DONE FOR JESUS?

❧ ❧ ❧

I walked a road of *make believe.*
I walked in dirt and worldly pleasures.
I walked wherever I felt pleased,
while God, my footsteps measured.

I took for me what e'er I wanted
to make for me a better life.
I never cared what I could do
about the work of Christ.

I let the world lead me along
and bragged how I loved God,
yet all the while my footsteps fell
on worldly paths . . . of earthen sod.

I want to walk like Peter did;
I want to walk on water.
I want to follow Jesus' call;
I want to walk like I oughtta.

I ought to do things differently;
I ought to care for others.
I ought to feed the Master's lambs;
my sisters and my brothers.

But what in me has magnified
the glory of the cross?
What have I done to lift up Christ,
no matter what the cost?

Oh, God please give me seeing eyes,
that fix themselves on You.
And let them see the work ahead,
to know what I can do.

Please let my eyes see only Christ
as He reaches out to me,
calming all my angry waves,
as I step into the sea.

That I might walk upon those waves
of pride and anger too,
putting them beneath my feet,
as I walk holy before You.

I want to leave the boat behind
with all it's worldly sin,
and feel You as You take my hand
and bid me enter in.

Please, help me Lord, to do the work
for You, God's precious Lamb,
who walked the surging seas
as well as Galilee's soft sand.

Show me how to follow, Lord,
and in my life's last setting sun,
let me hear You gently say,
"Come in . . .
I'm satisfied, My son."

SHOW ME

❧ ❧ ❧

I know you say you're a Christian
as you point toward the stars.
You say you have the love of God
but sir, I don't see that you are.

Your mouth often speaks without cleanness
but vulgarity isn't from Him.
And the way you treat others is not Love;
quite seriously, it's actually sin.

It's so confusing to hear you talk
about how you love the Lord
but showing the love of Jesus should not
be ignoring the sick and the poor.

How can you have a heart for God
and not be changed by His Grace?
If you really did love Jesus, our Lord,
it would show by a glow on your face.

What if God made the trees without leaves?
Where would the shade be then?
And how would the nests in the limbs be built
for the squirrels, the sparrows, and wrens?

And you might not know, it's the beautiful leaves
that remove the poison from the air.
It’s exchanged for pure, sweet oxygen
so all creatures can breathe everywhere.

A tree without leaves has nothing to show
nor can lay claim to being a tree,
and you, by your lack of acting like Christ
is showing the same thing to me.

Paul says if we are without any *love*
then all of our words are like brass,
tinkling and banging and clanging about,
proving our words to be trash.

"Show me," says James,
"what you're really made of."
Don't be just playing a game.
"Show me" that Jesus is really your Lord
when you walk the talk that you claim.

Clouds without water, being blown about
are like trees without leaves on the limb.
Words without action to prove what you say.
They don't *show* Jesus living within.

Show me your faith by your works, I say,
not by hollow words in the air.
Be a *doer* of the faith that you claim
by *showing* folks that you care.

Love them as Jesus would love them, I say.
Give forth to those in their need.
And the world will then see Jesus in you:
alive in your faith, and your deeds!

MARY HAD A PRECIOUS LAMB

❧ ❧ ❧

Mary had a little lamb;
its fleece was white as snow.
And everywhere that Mary went
the lamb was sure to go.

That version is from Mother Goose,
but here's another one.
It isn't cute or childish
and it isn't just for fun.

Mary had a precious Lamb,
more pure than driven snow.
But Mary knew before His birth,
she'd have to let Him go.

She followed Him to the Cross one day
and there she sat and cried,
'cause Mary's Lamb was killed, you see;
'twas for you and me He died.

I couldn't pay the price required;
my life was full of sin.
It took the perfect purest Lamb.
Jesus alone was Him.

Mary had a little Lamb,
that cried some in His sleep.
He then became a Shepherd,
and He cried o'er His lost sheep.

He is the Shepherd of the flock,
bringing us into the fold.
He is the Sheep-gate keeping us.
He picks us up to gently hold.

Mary had a little Lamb;
His love one day He'd show,
because as Shepherd of His sheep,
to Calvary He'd go.

He'd shed His blood instead of ours,
upon a cruel tree,
because the Lamb of God became
a Shepherd for you and me.

I need to be like Mary's Lamb,
and grow into a sheep.
I need to witness Jesus' love,
to all the people I meet.

I need to be a shepherd too,
and give my life for them.
I need to be just like my Lord,
by being a lamb like Him.

IS IT YOU?

❧ ❧ ❧

God is looking for a man . . .
A man to stand in the Gap.
Is it you?
There's someone that the Lord God needs
to fill a spreading crack.
Is it you?
God is looking for the one
to spread the message of His Son
Someone to tell it clear and true.
Is it you?
God is in need of that someone . . .
to take the Gospel Word.
Is it you?
God is searching for the one
who'll let his voice be heard.
Is it you?
Unless the Word is given out
and others have the chance to hear
the world will live and die in fear.
Is it you?
Isaiah said, "LORD here am I."
But there must be ONE more . . .
Is it you?
God needs a few good men to go
and give the world a chance to know.
Is it you?
His eyes are traveling to and fro;
He's looking for those few . . .
. . . Who will go? . . .
YOU KNOW! . . .
Is it you?

WE TRAVEL THE SAME ROAD

❧ ❧ ❧

One man goes East,
one man goes West.
The same road travel they both.

But the way they travel
and who goes with them
will determine where they go.

The same winds blow,
the same rains fall
upon two traveler's heads.

One man finds God,
the other rejects Him,
and travels to Hell at his death.
selah

TOO LATE

❧ ❧ ❧

At fourteen I thought I knew it all
I had all the time in this world,
just waiting at my fingertips
to do whatever I would do.

But then so soon I was thirty-six
and time was flying away.
Old age was racing at me so fast,
and I had played the fool.

"Too late, too late," I heard the clock
of time go whizzing by,
and God when called me I said "No"
tho' my last breath was near.

Then gasping on a bed of pain
and sickness . . . and torment
I realized that my life was gone,
and suddenly I knew fear.

"My God, what happens to me now?"
I thought that life would be
much slower and that I'd have time,
. . . plenty of time to wait.

But suddenly, no warning sound;
no horns, no clocks, no chimes.
I'm nearly in the hands of God,
and I'm afraid I'm late.

I didn't worry, didn't care,
that one day I would be,
standing in the presence of God,
facing eternity.

I always thought that I had time
to make those small decisions,
about eternity and such,
and what would happen then.

Because life didn't seem that fast
when I was having fun
but now
as I stare death in the face,
I don't know where it went.

"Tick Tock, Tick Tock,"
I hear the sound
of time now sweeping by,
and realize that very soon
I'll be there at the gate.

I've lived a fool in folly bent,
but now I see my plight.

"Tick Tock, Tick Tock,"
is there yet time,
or am I late,
too late,
too late?

CHRISTMAS IN HIS PRESENCE

❧ ❧ ❧

The tree is all trimmed in red, green, and gold.
We're glad that outside there is fresh fallen snow.
With lights all a-glitter and twinkling so bold,
we say we are thankful for Christmas.
Slippers for mother and warm gloves for dad.
Jimmy got the first bike he's ever had.
As they opened their gifts, everybody was glad.
But who thought about baby Jesus?

No room at the inn to lay His sweet head.
An old feeding trough to use for a bed.
I don't know that anyone ever heard said,
"Here is a King before us."

Our interest is centered on Saint Nick's bag of toys,
that we say are given to good girls and boys.
But amidst all the celebration and noise,
all we hear is Saint Santa Claus.
What happened to the songs that we used to sing
about the glad tidings the angels did bring;
about Bethlehem and the birth of a King,
who came down to Earth to save us?

We're so busy standing in great shopping lines,
after shopping for gifts so rare and so fine,
that the thought hardly ever enters into our mind:
Christmas is all about Jesus.

We're interested more in clothing and toys,
than we are in the virgin birth of a Boy,
who was born on a dirty sheep stall floor,
after leaving Heaven so precious.

Oh Lord, we have slipped so far away,
from the manger scene where the Baby lay,
when He came in such a miraculous way,
to lay His life down before us?

We care more about the presenting of things,
with shiny colors that whistle and ring,
than being in the presence of a heavenly King;
the presence of Holy King Jesus.

Oh, to spend an hour in those heavenly places,
and to see adoration on the angels' faces,
should make us want to hurry and hasten,
into the presence of Jesus.

But the presents and gifts become so important,
for daughter and uncle and brother and aunt,
that we begin telling ourselves we just can't
spend any of our time with Jesus.

There is no greater gift to receive
this Christmas than to humbly bow at His feet,
spending time in prayer and receiving His peace;
time in the presence of Jesus.

Forget the Christmas tree and the baseball.
Just quietly listen and answer the call
that God is sending out to us all:
"Spend this Christmas
in the presence of Jesus."

BATTLING THE DEMONS FROM HELL

❧ ❧ ❧

Thank you sir for being interested . . .
but yes I'm quite alright.
It's just that I've been through a lot;
that's why I look a fright.
You see, life used to be so normal.
Yeah, normal in every way.
But then I met some other members
of *the family* one day.

One by one they entered into
the life I loved so well.
And one by one they started me
on a lonely road to Hell.
But let me start at the starting place,
as innocent as can be
And tell you what this *family*
was able to do to me.

I was a doctor in my field.
I had a home and a wonderful wife,
until I brought somebody home
that started messing up my life.
I met *temptation* in my office
one bright and sunny day.
He really got my full attention
though he didn't have much to say.

So slowly, like a crawling worm
he wiggled up to my side,
and told me there were things I could do;
things to do and hide,
because they weren't anyone's business;
just between me and him,
and if I'd do these secret things
then he would be my friend.

He introduced me to *ol' drugs;*
a real close friend of his.
He said,
"*Ol' drugs* is a real cool guy
and after all, gee wiz,
a guy needs to have a little fun.
He can't be all work and no play."
Temptation was so convincing that
I didn't know what to say.

So I shook hands, hearing *drugs* say,
"Let's go. Let's have some fun!"
But even as I did what he said to do,
something inside of me went numb.
And as the days passed after that,
it seemed no matter where
I went I had a shadow, because
he was always there.

But *drugs* did keep his promise to me;
life became a ball,
because I found his friends and him
weren't so bad after all.
Then he introduced me to *pornography*
and *lust* at my beck and call.
And then *adultery* came in,
but I really didn't care at all.
My friends were showing me a side
of me I didn't know.
And soon my money was going fast
just like a mid-summer snow.
Then *gambling* started taking up
almost all of my time.
And time for my work and family
was falling far behind.

A twinge I had though--now and then--
about this new found life,
because I started to realize
I had no time for my wife.

You see, the friends I *thought* I had,
were not my friends at all,
for they came from another world
behind a mirrored hall.

Let me tell you what they did
in the mirror they reversed.
Everything they represented
was done by changing the words.
What we call bad they made look good;
not just good, but appealing.
They changed their looks and walk and talk
to mess up all my feelings.

They finally came out from the dark,
to guide me along the way,
into a *never-never-land*
without tomorrows or yesterdays.

Life was spinning far off course
with all my new found *friends,*
like *drugs, temptation, pornography,*
and partying without an end.

But, then one day they tired of me
because I was slowing down.
No longer could I pay the price
of carrying them around.
I said I wanted loose from them
to again go my separate way.
But oh how clear it then became,
the price I'd have to pay.

There was a battle line drawn for me
there in the sands of time;
a battle that I knew I'd lose
to these so called *friends* of mine.

Not just my money, not just fun,
not just my time, was their fee.
They gave me all they had to give
and they wanted all of me.

My brow now withered, worn, and drawn
by nights of worrying;
my bony frame, my weary mind,
my life laid to their claim.

I thought, if I could only raise
my will to fight this awful shame,
but now no longer could I think
clearly enough to know my name.

The battle lines were clearly drawn
and I was scared to death,
and then somebody breathed a name
that sounded like *Holiness.*
They called Him the *White Clad Warrior*
who had fought the very best.
Yes, He had fought and defeated
the best demons that were sent.

So in my anguish, hurt, and shame,
I called out one strong word,
and the *White Clad Warrior* came to destroy
with His sharp two-edg-ed sword.
Yes, He fought the battle in my place
and fought it very well,
killing the *Thief* of my peace, love, and joy,
along with the demons from Hell.

And when the battle was ended
and my peace and joy returned,
I saw Him sitting on a throne
bathed in the glory He had earned.
And angels were crying out so clear,
"Holy, holy to His name."
That's when I saw
the *White Clad Warrior*
and Jesus are the same.

So let me tell you the end of this story
that I love so very well.
If in your life you're fighting an army
of demons up from Hell,

don't try to do it all alone
and fight them with your weakened flesh.
No matter how strong or wise you are,
they'll use their very best.

And you alone will never win
against the power they send.
There will always be just one of you . . .
and a million or more of them.

You need the *White Clad Warrior;*
the Holy One from God,
for only Jesus can defeat
the one who dwells beneath the sod.

Down in the depths of Hell below
is the *Master* of the demons,
and he sends them up here into the air
with his deceitful scheming.

Messages from a burning Hell
sent by Satan himself,
while preparing a place for you down there
upon his trophy shelf.

So make the choice this very day.
Say, "I will not be his prize."
Just take a stand to defeat him
and make him realize,
the battle isn't yours alone,
it also belongs to Christ.
Tell him the *White Clad Warrior,* Jesus,
is fighting on your side.

Finally brethren, be strong in the Lord;
in the power of His might.
Put on the strong whole armor of God
against the Devil's wiles.
We wrestle not against flesh and blood
and things that we see well.
So call the *White Clad Warrior* to the fight
against your demons from Hell.

ANGELS OF CLAY

❧ ❧ ❧

Winging their way in wonderful circles,
angels descend to our world to be useful.
Out of the Heavens where they were created,
into our world as per God's approval,
come spiritual beings with mystical powers,
who eternally have been God's faithful followers.

And yet forgetting who they really are,
these created beings who have come from afar,
that we in amazement have all become blind
until they have captured our subconscious mind.

Until forms and images we have made them
created of clay again and again,
displayed on a mantel and shelves, to be seen,
as if we have bowed down upon bended knee,
to Satan, the angel who said, "Like God I will be!"
We allowed him to woo us; to herd us like sheep,
and to blow out our candles and put us to sleep.

A sleep of the ages, where we forget God,
who allowed His son Jesus to walk on this sod,
and be crucified, without love or respect,
while we worship things
made of porcelain instead.

We are caught up in clouds of this *angelic worship*
when only Christ Jesus, the Savior deserves it.
But one day in glory when anthems are raised,
we'll see real angels singing to Jesus . . .
their praise.

Then we'll be ashamed,
for the thousands of days
when we worshiped angels
which were just made of clay.

PRAYER

❧ ❧ ❧

Our Father which art in Heaven,
hallowed be Thy name;
Thy kingdom come, Thy will be done
on earth as it is in Heaven.

This is repeated over and over,
and over and over some more,
from lips of those both young and old,
from seven to seventy-four.
I say them too, in church sometimes,
or even at a meal.
So what's this fuss about prayers and praying?
What is this tension I feel?

I just don't have much time to waste
on sitting down and saying,
in some great formal form and pose,
"Well, here I am. I'm praying!"
I hear folks talking about prayer
and spending a lot of time
being lost so mystically,
while in their hour of quiet.
Well from what I hear of them professing,
it kinda seems that way,
but I think some of their *praying time* isn't
really what they say.
I wonder sometimes, "What are they thinking,
saying all those things?
Who can spend that much time praying,
down upon their knees?"
I think they just need attention
somewhere deep inside.
But hey, I'm stable; I'm O.K.
I have nothing to hide!
But never-the-less, since I'm talking
about that subject now,
sometimes inside I get a feeling,
of loneliness. You know how.

It's kinda like something missing;
something that's just undone.
But, hey. I know it's nothing spiritual;
I pray, like anyone.

What's that you say? You know the answer
to my predicament?
You think that you can tell which way
my spiritual man is bent?
Who? Satan fooling with my pride?
No, no, no. Oh no, you're wrong.
I go to church and read my Bible
and even sing the songs.
But . . . why am I sometimes so jealous
when I hear them say,
they have a *deep communion;*
a *conversation* when they pray?

Deep and peaceful, full of meaning;
something sweet and real;
something I don't get from praying;
something I don't feel.
It's like a horse that goes to water
and after a drink or two,
the water's gone, and he's still thirsty,
wondering what to do.
I go to pray and say some words,
but they don't seem to flow.
They just get stuck down in my throat,
without a place to go.
Sometimes I'm bruised and beaten down
and need to talk to God,
while deep inside a voice tells me
my prayers are just a *facade.*
I can't get on His *hot-line*
'cause my telephone is broken,
and I can't tap His holy power
with prayers that are just tokens.
Just tokens of a prayer life;
tokens of what it should be;
a little mumble here and there;
that's all He gets from me,

thrown out to the God of Heaven.
It’s like a little crumb.
Can it be that's what I'm doing?
Am I really all that dumb?
If dumbness means that I don't speak
enough in prayerful words,
then dumb I am, compared to those
whose prayer life I have heard.

They spend those long sweet hours of prayer
in a closet where they hide.
Perhaps they're right, perhaps I'm stumbling,
over my own willful pride.
Perhaps they're also right about
me being spiritually blind.
And Satan working through my pride
has stolen precious time;
time that should be spent with Jesus,
fellowshipping one to one;
pride that blocks my line of prayer
to the resurrected Son.

Oh God, if my poor lips are feeble,
unaccustomed to holy words,
lift them up Lord, give them courage,
from now on to be heard.
And if my hands are hanging down,
lift them, Lord, in prayer and praise,
pointing to the cross of Calvary,
where the Savior bore my shame.
And Lord, if my dark mind is busy,
encumbered with the cares of Earth,
lift it up Lord; pour it out; freshen it like a holy birth.
Oh God, if my cold heart is weary,
lift it up with love anew;
first for Jesus, then for others.
Teach it how to love like You.
Oh God, if my voice is frail,
use it any way You can.
And Lord if I have so wandered
then please take me by my hand.

Even if my prayer is small, Lord,
lift it up to Heaven's portals,
then lift me Lord, when I'm praying,
far above the realm of mortal;
far above the lure of living;
far above the clutch of pride.
Bring me to Your royal presence,
oh, my Lord, where You abide.
Give me, Lord, what e'er those saints have,
during quiet times spent there.
Oh, God, within the halls of glory,
will You please lead me in prayer.

Please forgive sarcastic words, Lord,
sent like arrows from my tongue,
against the saints who bowed in prayer
while I was bent on having fun.
And yes, oh God, a life of prayer,
I believe can still be mine,
when I learn to run the race
carrying not the weight of pride.
Lord, I stand before you naked,
shamefully knowing who I am.
Please forgive me precious Father,
and please remember, I'm just a man.
Yes, like Adam in the garden,
I have let the serpent in,
eaten of his fruit of pride,
and swallowed down his taste for sin.
So God, I'm asking You to destroy
in me this awful sin of mine.
Teach me Lord, to pray like You did,
long ago in . . . time.
Let me feel Your holy presence
as I come to the throne of grace.
Oh God, that I might get a glimpse
into Your precious, holy face.
While lifting up to You, my mouth,
and asking, if You to fill
it with humility in prayer,
Lord, pleasing to Your will.

IS SALVATION FREE?

❧ ❧ ❧

There is a story written in blood,
at the foot of the cross where there came a flood.
Abundant salvation offered so free;
given without cost; purchased for me.

Unchangeably changed by the Spirit divine.
Hallelujah, Jesus is mine!

Shackles all gone and forever I'm free,
paid for by His blood, and given to me.
The thorns of His crown beaten into His head;
feet nailed to the cross, now covered in red.
As long as I live I will be His.
Saved by the precious blood that He shed.

He came to die and pay for my sin.
How could I not want to let Him come in?
To keep me forever from burning in Hell;
how could I not want His story to tell?

He said He'd give *life forever* to me.
and from my sinfulness, I'd be set free.
But yes, it would cost me something, He said;
cost me my everything, feet to my head.
He said His death would stand in my place,
and all of my sinfulness would be erased.
But sin must be paid so He paid it for me,
wiping away all the debt of my deeds.

Then in the place of a debt that was mine,
He'd fill even me with His Glory divine.
And then I could tell the world what He'd done;
how He died for me . . .
Him . . .
God's only son.

I thought it was too late for me.
I'd already been sentenced, I hadn't a plea.
Then Jesus came and freed me instead,
hanging there crucified, 'tho he was dead.

What can I pay Him now that He's gone?
gone into Heaven with the heavenly throng,
watching o'er me living down here below?
How can I pay Him? It's my life that I owe.

So yes, I will serve Him in life and in deed.
"Let me serve my Savior," is now my heart's plea.
Visions of mercy come into my mind,
of my crucified Savior now in Heaven, alive.

Yes, nailed there He died, on Calvary's tree,
but out of the tomb He brought victory.
Salvation was purchased though He was dead.
Resurrection the proof,
'cause He rose like He said.
This is His story written in blood,
at the foot of the cross where there came a flood.
Abundant salvation given to me;
purchased at His cost; purchased for me.

And now I am changed
and He's unchangeably mine.
Hallelujah, Jesus is my story divine.
Shackles all gone and forever I'm free,
paid for by His blood, and given to me.

What did it cost Him? It cost Him His all.
Could I give him less than what He'd ask for?
Yes, I will serve Him for pardoning me,
because I understand that salvation's not free.

I gave up my sin; He gave His life.
He gave up glory; I give up my pride.
He bought with His blood, a pardon for me,
so I'll give Him my all;
Salvation's not free.

This is His story written in blood,
at the foot of the cross where there came a flood.
Abundant salvation given so free;
given without cost; purchased for me.

As long as I live now I will be His
saved by the blood that my Jesus shed.
From thorns in the crown
beaten into His head;
feet nailed to the cross,
now stained in red.
I'm unchangeably changed
by His spirit divine.
Hallelujah, Jesus is mine!
Shackles all gone
and forever I'm free,
paid for by His blood,
and given to me.

If you'll count the cost then you'll understand,
there is a price.
Your life is demanded.

He paid the full price.
He paid the fee.
Now He deserves everything.

No, salvation's not free.
But yes, it's a bargain,
for you and for me . . .

AMAZED AM I

❧ ❧ ❧

How utterly amazed am I
when e'er I gaze into the sky,
and see the clouds so billowy
which float about so I can see,
the beauty of them as they are;
companions of the gleaming stars
which fill the night with majesty,
for all who take the time to see
the beauty that was given us,
to hopefully look up.
Who can deny the beauty there
suspended in the heavenly air,
where though mere man can never go
yet he can watch the heavenly show,
where fluffy clouds make such a view
suspended in the sky of blue.
Why should we waste the beauty then
of what should be seen by all men,
amazing as is meant to be
and printed on our memory.
So, when we age as all will do
we might believe that me and you
in our last hour we then may fly
upwards to be clouds in the sky,
and those below will take our place
to gaze up utterly amazed.

SHADOWS IN THE DARK

❧ ❧ ❧

There is a road so long and lonely.
Sometimes I sit and think, "If only . . .
If only I'd never the journey begun,
perhaps much happier I'd be."

But, who can say, on the day we start,
pure of soul and brave of heart;
on pathway not clear, seen only in part,
who can know where the journey would go?

Just putting my footprints upon the sand,
one foot in front of the other and,
making a mark in the long road of time
not being sure where it will go.

Will it take me places I've not been before,
while darkness closes all around
and blinds these eyes of which way to go?

The sands have led me down and down,
to deepening, darkness all around
'til I'm underground in a deep dark pit;
nowhere to run and nowhere to sit.

I cannot run and I cannot stay
because it's way too dark to see.
My mind is whirring and all I can say is,
"Is this eternity?"

Is this eternity forevermore?
I'm walking in darkness; never sure
of what is ahead for me.
Is this darkness eternity?

Total darkness like I'm blind,
doing strange things, tricking my mind.
I can't even see my hand, oh God.
Do you have an answer for me?

No sky, no ground, no floor, no wall;
nothing but darkness forevermore.
It's only God who I can call.
Oh God, help me out of this darkness!

Then like a veil where there was none,
I think I vaguely see someone,
or is it just a shadow there?
A shadow in the dark?

No . . . this is blackness,
black as can be;
it covers and even smothers me.
I know that its impossible to see . . .
SHADOWS in the dark.

But yes! I do see something there;
not actually SEE, but yet I know,
it's brilliant and fair,
believing . . . it is meant for me.
And then a shape like God himself . . .
How would I know? I cannot tell.
I only know that HE has come for me.

Then suddenly a brilliant light,
beamed into my darkened pit,
destroying darkness
where once my foot had slipped.
Now framed by light I see Him come:
Gods one and only, brilliant Son;
more brilliant than the sky above,
answering my plea.

Darkness, darkness, long and lonely,
but then I called the one and only
who is in control,
who even makes shadows in the dark.
Now light so brilliant, white and fair,
fills my world both out and in,
because the Son of God has come
and made my pathway sure.

O friend, if you walk dark and lonely,
sometimes thinking, "Oh, if only . . .
If only I had never started,
perhaps I'd be much happier."
Then look for Jesus on that dark day.
Give him full control in every way.
He will bring light into the darkness
and lift you from the pit.
And suddenly the brilliant light
of Jesus will fill your heart,
and impossible things you'll begin to see,
His light so pure
will even cause shadows . . .
shadows in the dark.

A VESSEL OF HONOR

❧ ❧ ❧

Silver and gold have I none,
But such as I have give I thee.
In the name of Jesus Christ of Nazareth,
rise up and walk with me.

As silver is dug from the Earth far below,
so God digs deep to rescue a soul.
As silver is crushed and melted and poured,
so man is transformed as he yields to the Lord.

Tried by the fires of redeeming grace,
God melts the heart of the poor human race.
As I see what He gave on Calvary,
humbled I am by what He did for me.

Broken was Christ where I should have been.
Crushed for the whole world to pay for my sin.
Melted and poured in what seemed to be waste,
He took the refining fire in my place.

Into the fire of man's hate and scorn,
went Christ the Savior, God's only born,
to purify me from shame and from sin,
into the fire my Savior went in.

But now God in love wants to put me in too,
so I can be part of what Jesus went through.
And the refiners fire will burn from within,
the dross and the waste from my life of sin.

Heat me oh God, in the refiners fire,
burn out the man who has lived as a liar.
Refine me as silver for your holy use.
Refine me in fires of Your holy truth.
Make me oh God, as a vessel worthwhile,
made of pure silver, crucified in Your fire.
Melt me and pour me, make me Your own.
Use me oh God, near to Your holy throne.

SORRY, I NEVER KNEW YOU

❧ ❧ ❧

Last night as I lay sleeping,
a dream came to me
I dreamed about the end of time,
about eternity
I saw a million sinners,
fall on their knees to pray
The Lord just sadly shook His head,
and this I heard Him say:

***"Sorry, I never knew you.
Depart from Me for ever more.
Sorry, I never knew you.
Ggo and serve the one you served before."***

I thought the time had fully come,
that I must stand my trial
I told the Lord that I had been
a Christian all the while.
Through His book He took a look,
and sadly shook His head.
He placed me over on His left
and this I heard Him say:

**"Sorry, I never knew you.
I find no record of your birth.
Sorry, I never knew you.
Go and serve the one
that you served down on earth."**

There were my wife and children;
I heard their loving voice.
They must have been so happy.
Oh how they did rejoice.
With robes of white around them,
their faces all aglow,
my little girl looked up at me
and said with sadness in her voice:

"Daddy, we can't go with you.
We must stay here on this beautiful shore.
Sorry, for we still love you.
But you can not be our Daddy anymore."

And when I had awakened,
with tears still in my eyes
I brushed them all away and saw
much to my surprise,
my loving wife and babies,
and I knew I'd had a dream
so down upon my knees I fell,
and for mercy I did plead:

**"Father, Who art in Heaven,
I know You gave Your only Son.
Father, please forgive me.
I want to be Yours when You come."**

THE DAY THE SKY FELL

❧ ❧ ❧

The day was beautiful with a clear blue sky.
Not a care in my heart; not a cloud in my eye.
I wasn't even thinking about Heaven or hell.
I wonder if God was . . . the day the sky fell?

I always thought there was plenty of time,
so life for me was wonderfully sublime.
I did in my own peace and comfort dwell,
until that one day . . . when the sky fell.

But, I don't want to get ahead of the tale.
If I do that, the story surely will fail.
So let me go back to the beginning for you,
And we'll read every page, as we're supposed to . . .

In the beginning when God was all alone,
sitting somewhere on His big royal throne,
He said, "There is something I will do by and by.
I'll create an earth, moon, and sun, in the sky."

Although it had never been done before,
God rolled up His sleeves and got to the chore.
"Let Earth have a form. Let water appear.
Be animals and man be together, without fear."

And then in the process as six days went by,
with only His Words coming down from the sky,
God made everything just as He choose to:
grass, earth, trees and sky, and then me and you.

Out of the darkness that was shapeless and twisted;
down from the sky where nothing existed,
God put it in place by the sound of His voice,
and made it all good, according to His own choice.

Well, years passed away and then a problem arose,
when some rebellious angels became God's foes.
They followed a leader who had appointed himself,
right out of the place that God gave them to dwell,

to arise in rebellion and take over God's throne,
for Lucifer, the beautiful one, to have as his own.
But oh, what an error they made on that day,
believing that God, would let them have their own way.

God said, "How from Heaven thou art fallen, oh Lucifer.
You, the son of the morning, how could you do so?
Thou said in thine heart, 'I will sit on God's throne',
tho' I'd already given you one of your own."

Was there fighting and war up in Heaven above?
Did God forgive them all, and shower them with love?
Oh no, God made them a place He called Hell,
and from Heaven to there, from the sky they all fell.

God said, "Down to the side of the pit you all go;
down to the place I've prepared far below;
down to the place that I've made called Hell."
And that's what happened, the first time the sky fell.

But mankind still listened to what Lucifer said,
as he poured out his lies to our heart and our head,
so that we wouldn't listen to what God wanted for us,
but we latched on to greed and murder and lust.

So once again God had to help the poor man,
and He drew up His heartbreaking *sacrifice-plan.*
He'd send down His Son to die on a cross,
to protect us from Satan and from eternal loss.

Born as a babe, to be like you and me,
He agreed to be crucified, on a cross carved tree,
as God showed us the way with His eternal love,
and He sealed it in Heaven by His only Son's blood.

Hanging in agony for my sin, pain, and strife,
Jesus gave up the ghost . . . He gave up his life.
As the sky opened up and there fell from above,
the signature of God, on the wings of a dove.

But then in the year of two-thousand-and-one,
the day of September eleven, would come,
and the dreams of Satan to rule o'er the skies,
would cause thousands of innocent people to die.

As out of the skies like mad demons from Hell,
three missiles from Satan destructively fell,
to pour out his anger on the inhabitants of Earth,
and to bring in the terror of the *end-times birth.*

He commandeered planes, and the minds of weak men,
and at the great cities he'd steer them again,
where thousands of unsuspecting people dwell,
to be killed by his anger on that day the sky fell.

In Isaiah fourteen, Satan cried out loud,
"I *will* ascend above the heights of the clouds."
And he didn't care that millions would die,
to fulfill his dream to be like the Most High.

"Is this the man that made the Earth to tremble;
is this the same man that made kingdoms to shake?"
Yes, he may have power, but not over Heaven.
He isn't God. He's a miserable fake!

The Bible says heathen will scream in their rage,
and kingdoms will fear, and tremble, and shake.
But God by an utterance, will make everything melt,
as His majestic power, by all will be felt.

Yes, the sky did come down by God's all divine hand,
when He created Earth and all things by His plan.
And again it was used to transport Satan's mob,
down into their Hell, by the power of God.

Then God in the form of Christ Jesus His Son,
was blessed with a blessing in the form of a dove.
But there's coming a day more awesome than these,
when the skies will break open and out of the east,

Jesus Christ will ascend with an army unnumbered.
And with sin, death and Hell, be no longer encumbered,
He'll bring the great story that eternity will tell,
of how magnificent He was the day the sky fell.

How He fought the great battle for you and for me,
and then Hell, death and sin no longer would be.
And the war cry of Heaven will be heard by all,
on that glorious day when the sky will fall.

As a child, there's a fairy tale I used to hear,
told about a chicken that cried out in fear,
as it ran into town, it's story to tell,
crying, "Look what happened to the sky. It fell!"

Well, an acorn had fallen upon its little head,
so it thought it was in danger of soon being dead.
"Oh, the sky is falling," the little chicken did tell,
but this was a child's tale, about when the sky fell.

But eons from now there's a true story we'll tell,
how Satan was defeated with all his angels from Hell.
My heart burns within me to ask you dear friend,
"Where will *your* place of existence be then?"

When God clearly says, "Enough is enough;
I've waited and waited, now it's time to get tough."
And out of the Heavens with trump and with sword,
on a Warriors horse, Jesus comes with His Word.

And all of the armies that Satan has borne,
will die with their master to whom they were sworn,
by sin and rebellion and hope with out hope,
the field will be filled by their bloodied corpse.

But God's men, the *saved ones,* by His holy grace,
will ascend through the skies into His holy place.
But others, with Satan, will go down to Hell,
and we'll each have much different stories to tell.

We'll say, "The day was beautiful with a clear blue sky.
Not a care in my heart, not a cloud in my eye.
I wasn't even thinking about Heaven or Hell,
but God certainly was, the day the sky fell."

Some will say, "I thought I had plenty of time,
so life for me was wonderfully sublime.
Yes, in my own peace and comfort I dwelt,
until that great day, when the sky fell."

Now you have a choice to make, precious one,
because in the near future, it's going to come.
There'll be stories of Heaven, and stories of Hell.
Which story will you have, about the day the sky fell?

Oh, that the sky would break open again.
Oh, that it would enter the hearts of all men.
Yes, this is the story of God's great Love to tell,
from Calvary's hill, the day the sky fell.

*** * ***

Now you have a choice to make precious one,
because in the future, it's going to come.
There'll be stories of Heaven,
and stories of Hell.
Which story will you have
about the day the sky fell?

Even so . . . come Lord Jesus . . .
Revelation 22:20

BY CHOICE

❧ ❧ ❧

Filled with my self, I just wandered the world,
feasting on life, leaving no stone unturned.
But the joy that I wanted was not to be had,
'cause all of my living left me empty and sad.

Unpleasant affairs lining up end to end,
'til I couldn't remember where it all had began.
Dark alleys, motel rooms, of drugs and despair.
It all left me empty thinking, "God is unfair."

Why doesn't He treat me like others I know:
lives full of sunshine; a wonderful glow
they seem to have something that I haven't found,
while they seem to fly, I'm so earthly bound.

I thought that just giving my life to the Lord,
was a really big deal; 'twas all I could afford.
What else did he want? I had nothing to give.
Yet I knew this wasn't the way I should live.

And then as I wandered the back streets one night,
dirty and broke; a disgusting old sight,
I heard somewhere nearby, a heart touching sound,
and nearing the corner, I stepped on around.

And there to the sidewalk, a wide open door
where people were welcoming the sick and the poor.
And an old preacher man was singing a song;
a song about Jesus. Oh, it had been so long.

So long since I'd heard the sweet words of my youth.
So long since I'd thought about words full of truth.
So long, I'd forgotten, what a heart really craves.
So long that I thought, "Does Jesus still save?"

I stood and listened, to that preacher sing,
and my sin dried soul began to drink in
the words of assurance, that Jesus loves me,
and that He would wash me, in His purity.

"Dying with Jesus, by death reckoned mine.
Living with Jesus, a new life divine.
Looking to Jesus 'til glory doth shine.
Moment by moment, oh Lord I am thine . . ."

And the preacher came near at the end of the song,
and taking my arm he said,
"Son you've been wrong.
The love and the joy that you're looking for
will never be found on a barroom floor.
All over the world like you, I have trod,
searching and wondering,
"Where is my God?"
And an old-time preacher told me where to start.
He said God's truth was settled deep in my heart.
But it was so dirty, and filled with my sin,
that I knew there wasn't room for Him to come in.
My heart was so hard, like a dirty ole stone
that Jesus would never want me for His own.
Then God gave me this song in the midst of that storm,
and my cold heart changed, and was suddenly warm.
I've been singing it since because my God is real,
and it's something the world doesn't want you to feel.

Then the preacher said, "How much more can you take
if God sends you into that fiery ole lake?
The one that lost souls follow Satan into;
the one that might be, ahead just for you."

I didn't answer;
I just went on inside,
and went to the front of that place,
and I cried.
I told God I wanted that ole preacher's joy;
something I hadn't known,
since I was a boy.

Then I felt a clean washing all over my soul,
and for the first time in years, I really felt whole.
I knew that God wasn't mine to have just for a day,
but for moment by moment, in every way.

I made a decision to pray and to read,
and God's given me all of the peace that I need.
He washed me and cleansed me, in His purity,
and if you want to find me, here's where I'll be:

At the foot of the cross,
where He pardoned my sin;
at the foot of the cross,
where Jesus came in.
No more dark alleys
or sad lonely nights.
I found joy in Jesus,
and I chose Him as mine.

THE LIGHTHOUSE

❧ ❧ ❧

Over the land and out to sea,
A beaming brightness of light can be seen,
crowning the waves with a brilliant white,
to help the sea-tossed sailors at night,
far out on the ocean.

Fighting the fears and perils there,
from biting darkness of night everywhere.
Without a hope of e'er being saved,
from the dark of this fearful place,
where fear is the only emotion.

Oh how many a life has been seen,
to be swept away to an eternity,
of void and darkness everywhere,
to never again see the loving face;
gone forevermore.

Oh that a light in the darkness may,
be placed somehow to show the way;
a way to find shelter and peace and hope,
and tied with a cord of strong faithful rope,
there on a warm, peaceful shore.

The ships are so torn and tossed about,
by the power the ocean so wildly flouts,
causing many to sink sadly there,
ending in sorrowful lonely despair,
where a life is torn apart.

While somewhere in sadness a Captain cries,
"Hold on, hold on, and look for the light!
Thus cometh our source. Don't give up on help.
Steer hard for the light beyond yonder swell,
and the Light from God's own heart."

Why do we linger and fight the swells?
Why so determined to go down to Hell,
when His light so faithfully shines the way
o'er each tem-pest-u-ous crushing wave?
The light has shown His devotion.

There stands the lighthouse of Jesus Christ.
For years he's been reaching toward mankind.
The light of God's love hung atop a hill,
calling, "Come to my safety if you will,
out of the worldly ocean."

Over the land and out to sea,
the brightness of His light can still be seen,
crowning the waves with a brilliant white,
to help the sin tossed sailors at night,
drowning in the waters of sin.

Stop fighting the fears and perils out there.
The Lighthouse will calm your every care.
Come to the Captain and be fully saved,
from the ocean of sin so dark with despair,
where the light of His Love takes you in.

THE RACE

❧ ❧ ❧

I've sat in the bleachers
a long, long time,
knowing that the race
should also be mine.

So I'm going to get busy
and take my spiritual part,
to show all those who also run
that I will do my part.

This is a brand new year to live,
I'm going to give it my all.
I'm going to trust my God to keep me
from tiring and taking a fall.

This is Christian determination
that you see upon my face.
I've made up my mind I'm going in.
Yes, I'm entering the race.

Give me faith Lord, give me faith,
and endurance that will last,
and Lord, don't let me focus
on my failures from the past.

Give me love Lord, give me love,
before I start to run,
and give a sense of urgency.
This isn't just for fun.

Help me run Lord, help me run,
help me keep reaching forth;
contending for the mark ahead
and run for all I'm worth.

Give me souls Lord, give me souls,
to lay at Jesus' feet.
Let me win them from the world
of all the lost souls that I meet.

Help me, the Breath of Life, to pass
to those who are next in line.
That it may put strength in their heart
just as You gave to mine.

The grand prize isn't always given
to the fleet of foot.
But often it is given to those
who faithfully endure.

Help me to be the example, Lord
for those who are ahead,
that running as Your champion
is not a thing to dread.

Give me souls Lord, give me souls,
to lay at Jesus' feet.
Let me talk about Jesus
to everyone I meet.

Help me Lord to share the Gospel
right in the Devils face.
Oh dear Jesus, help me be
Your runner in this spiritual race.

* * *

It's time to stretch; share your love.
It's time to trust your faith.
It's time to give the bleachers up.
It's time to run the race.

THE BANK OF ETERNITY

❧ ❧ ❧

I've worked so hard these many years
and yet don't seem to have,
enough of anything to keep,
for future needs and such.
Like last week's check, it disappeared
before the bills were paid,
and now the mortgage company
is making quite a fuss.

But that's the way of this old world.
It never seems to change.
It's work and pay, and work and pay;
eternally in debt.
It seems no matter what I do
I just can't meet the ends.
And try as I might I can't seem
to ever get ahead.

I put it in the bank and then
I take it out again.
It's, "Fill out the deposit slip,"
and then, "Write out a check."
I'm always way behind my needs,
no matter what I do.
Why should I try? Why should I care?
I'm just a nervous wreck.

But then I thought about a word
I read once in the Bible,
about a way to put away
and keep a treasure sure.
I put into the hands of God
those things I cherish most,
like kindness, love, and mercy
to make my account secure.

And when upon the Judgement Day
my settling time has come,
a bank account to draw upon
will be there in my name.
. . . And I can stand before my Lord
there in the heavenly bank,
and He will say,
"Welcome. Well done."
And I won't be ashamed.

Because of what I've done on earth
I'll have security
laid up for me to rest upon,
in the Bank of Eternity.

A PARENT'S HEART

❧ ❧ ❧

I know she breaks your heart in two,
because of how she's living,
but have you prayed for her?
And yes, I know about your son,
and all the pain he's giving.
But have you prayed for him?

God answers prayer at night or noon
and all times in between.
There's not a moment of the day
when He will not be seen.
But why cry to the Lord at all
with burdens, pains and cares,
unless you've spent some time with Him,
upon your knees in prayer?

What right have you expecting God
to save your wayward child,
who's running through the streets of life
recklessly and wild,
if you are guilty of not praying
against their way of sin
and you are guilty of not spending
time in prayer with Him.

If you're not spending time with him
the way you ought to do,
then as a careless child of God,
you're being wayward too.

Do you really want your daughter
saved from living wrong?
Well, have you held her up to God
in prayer the whole night long?
Does your son need Jesus, but,
he's headed down to Hell?
Then, does your heart cry out for him
from the depths of your *prayer-well?*

When children are no longer playing
in their own back yard,
they need a Christian parent,
to pray while standing guard.

This day, this hour, this moment, Mother,
is the time to start,
to reach the Lord in Heaven, Father,
with a praying parent's heart.

It's more than shelter that they need
on any given day.
They need you more than just a meal.
They need to know you pray.

* * *

**I know she breaks your heart in two,
because of how she's living,
but have you prayed for her?
And yes, I know about your son,
and all the pain he's giving.
But have you prayed for him?**

THE MODERN CHURCH

❧ ❧ ❧

I borrow these words from years gone by;
from a past that is now nearly gone,
when visions of church would come to me,
as Momma would sing them to us in a song.
"Oh, come to the church in the valley;
Oh, come to the church in the vale.
No spot is so dear to my childhood,
as the little brown church in the dale."

But where is the feeling of comfort now,
that I used to feel in my breast?
As I pictured it back in my childhood when,
the Church was a place of sweet rest

And there on a bright Sunday morning
as we listened to the bells sharply toll,
the air all around was gently transformed,
into peace that the world would behold.

But today in the new light of morning,
from a bright, shiny, white limousine,
we stride into brass, glass, and marble,
in the Church where we want to be seen.

Where the tapestries are all made of velvet,
and displayed over walls decked in gold,
while crystal chandeliers make a statement,
where the simple love story should be told.

Is it only by man's hand of fortune,
that the Church-house can preach it today?
Or would it be better to hear it
in a chapel constructed of clay?

Then . . . it used to be that the Church-house
drew crowds from the rich and the poor,
but today, if we don't put a *show* on,
they won't even darken the door.

When spiritual pollution's the solution,
and the fire we no longer desire,
God will write "Ichabod" on the church door,
and no longer will He come inside.

Oh, why has the church of my childhood,
snuggled there in the valley below,
now been changed into one on a hilltop,
dressed up like an actor in a show?

Church, remember, that God said from Heaven,
He would rather you were hot or cold
like the little brown church in the valley,
I remember from those days of old.

But today we have heard the world speaking,
who demands that we do it their way,
and lukewarmness has entered the Church-house,
leaving God on the outside to say:

"Come ye all, come all that are hungry;
come ye all, who are weary and tired.
There is still the brown church in the valley,
and you're welcome to come on inside.
But leave all your *works* on the outside,
and be satisfied when you come in,
with the old Holiness of Gods Word,
'til the heart is convicted of sin."

And you'll have to leave all of the trimmings,
made of velvet, and silver, and gold,
to be satisfied with the old Gospel,
where the story of Christ is still told.

BESIDE THE BITTER WATERS

❧ ❧ ❧

"Sing ye to the Lord,
for He hath triumphed gloriously.
Yea, the horse and rider
He hath thrown into the sea."

The enemy said I will pursue,
and I will overtake.
I will kill them with my sword,
yea, their destruction I will make.
But God blew with His mighty wind
upon the open sea,
and closed the waters there again
upon the enemy.

Bitter was the battle
that ole Pharoah would have fought,
but God's children walked upon dry land
as if there was a drought.

"Sing ye to the Lord,
for He hath triumphed gloriously.
Yea, the horse and rider
He hath thrown into the sea."

Bitter were the waters
they found on the other side,
even though the Lord destroyed
the enemy in the tide.

So Israel grumbled hatefully,
while Moses prayed, "Dear Lord, show me
what I'm supposed to do with them.
Instruct me with Your word."

They couldn't drink the water
for it's bitterness.
God had Moses cut a tree
and make the waters blessed.

"Sing ye to the Lord,
for He hath triumphed gloriously.
Yea, the horse and rider
He hath thrown into the sea."

Pharaoh rode a horse into
a battle he could not win.
God closed the sea upon him
burying him and all his men.

The enemy behind them,
the waters then turned sweet,
as Pharaoh and his army
were cast into the sea.

Now Israel sings a new song
and it's easy to repeat.
It's found in the Old Testament
Exodus, chapter fifteen:

"Sing ye to the Lord,
for He hath triumphed gloriously.
Yea, the horse and rider
He hath thrown into the sea."
Exodus 15:21-25

Now Jesus asks for you to trust Him
to do the same for you.
Don't you think that trusting Him
is the least that you could do?

He gave His life. He bled and died.
He paid for all your sins.
Will you ask Christ into your life
and put your trust in Him?

Please,
with your head bowed, and you mind clear of all else,
will you simply ask Jesus to forgive you of all your sins
and come into your heart,
and accept you to be His own child.
He really does want you to be His,
and He will be yours.

DANCING WITH THE DEVIL

❧ ❧ ❧

Bright lights and country music,
or maybe it's rock and roll?
The cigarette smoke and alcohol
will soon be taking its toll.

A dangerous place to do your dancing,
thinking it's fun and free,
but sooner than you had ever imagined,
you're paying a sad penalty.

Dangerously we dance through the world,
lured by its bright array
of blinking signs that light up the night,
and temptations that hide in the day.

Invisibly the tempter is there;
the Devil, the destroyer of souls,
as he slyly seduces poor mankind
to come dance in the danger zone.

With a musical beat, the laughter rings,
and hides the enemy's plan,
to make you a captive in his Hell,
ruled by his hideous hand.

Where is this danger zone, you ask,
from which I should depart?
My friend, it's where you'd least suspect.
It's deep within your heart.

A heart unyielded, dancing free
obeying its own will;
a heart once lost in the danger zone,
is a soul that Satan can kill.

Jesus tells us, "Be afraid,
dancing in the danger zone,
where Satan has the power to kill,
the body and the soul."

Leave now, today, while there is time,
before God rings the bell,
when those caught in the danger zone,
will dance into Satan's Hell.

But when the dancing is all done,
and eternity begins,
you'll realize that all his lies
have trapped you in deadly sin.

The danger zone will be passed away,
and death will take its place,
so why not turn to Jesus now,
and accept His saving grace?

Turn your back on Satan's music.
Turn and dance away.
Dance right out of the danger zone,
and into God's arms today.

THE CROSS AT GROUND ZERO

❧ ❧ ❧

The day was dreary and I had nothing to do.
I felt empty, which was normal as can be.
I knew Sabbath was coming in just a few days,
but it really wasn't interesting to me.

I was hoping for an excuse to keep me away,
'cause inside I just didn't care.
Then I heard the crowd yelling so I ran along,
to see what was happening there.

They were pushing a bloodied man down the street.
Just another criminal, I guess.
But something about Him caught and held my attention.
He was somehow different from the rest.

Then the hammer was striking the rough metal spikes,
as they nailed Him by wrists and by feet.
And again I was taken by the way He submitted.
Who was this man I didn't meet?

And as the cross raised and it took Him aloft,
I saw majesty in His beaten face.
As He died He said, "Father, forgive them for this."
And someone cried out, "He died in MY place."

The centurion who gambled for, and won His clothes,
was saying that something was odd.
Then suddenly realization shone on his face,
and he said, "Surely, He's the Son of our God . . ."

The crowd walked away and the place was now quiet,
so I went closer, to look at this man.
And as I knelt before Him, though He was dead,
I experienced something amazing, first hand.

Love flowed out from Him that reached into my soul,
'til my loneliness and fear was all lost.
Then I looked at my hands and my knees where I knelt
in His blood, at the foot of the cross.

From the first I saw Him, I wanted to know Him,
and now I was sure that I could,
if I'd always remember that Ground Zero experience,
where He hung on that rough piece of wood.

But I also met me, the one He died for,
and though I am unworthy I accepted this man.
From the cross at Ground Zero I looked up and saw,
that His life for mine, was His plan.

I looked once again at that torn, bloody face,
and I knew that I'd found my real hero.
The Son of God, Jesus, my Savior from sin,
whom I met on the cross at Ground Zero.

THE UNCHANGING GOD

❧ ❧ ❧

I was born so helpless,
so needy and weak,
that for years on other
people I leaned.
And you . . . just like me,
grew as days became years,
and we grew up to be
either loving or mean.
Our bones and our muscles
grew depending on food,
while our character and mind
became both bad and good,
so we started NOT doing
the things that we should,
with a changeable style
and a changeable mood.

Changes in time . . . changes in seasons . . .
changes in me without rhyme or a reason.
I am so glad that when times are unstable,
there is One I can count on who ALWAYS is able.
The world that was young once,
like me . . . has grown old.
Sheep now grow in cages, instead of the fold.
Jet planes sail the skies like the ships on the sea,
and what's yet in the future is too scary for me.

But there in the Heavens beyond man and machine
is a wonder that no human eye has yet seen.
There the unchanging God that created it all
sits high on his throne, so dependable; supreme.
Oh, but words don't exist to describe Majesty,
or to tell how my heart knows that He will love me,
no matter how often I wander or change,
He's more solid than any rock ever could be.

For the buildings will crumble
and my world will explode,
and the things that once were,
we will no longer hold,
because nothing is stable,
there is nothing that lasts,
except the unchanging God
who holds future and past.
Thankful I am,
for when I'm laid 'neath the sod,
He will look to His angels,
and give them a nod,
and to an unchanging world
I will be called to come,
by the unchanging
God . . .
Holy Spirit . . .
and Son . . .

ALMOST

❧ ❧ ❧

I wonder what the snow looks like
and the sparkling of the rain
as it lights upon the window
and runs down the window pane?

I'll bet the sun is very warm
when the morning brings its light,
pushing away the darkness
that hides everything at night.

And I can only imagine
what it must feel like to be
cuddled up to Momma's breast
while I sit upon her knee.

You see I've looked so forward to
having all these things,
like seeing light and shadows
and hearing robins sing.

I guess I'll just imagine
how my cheeks would feel to blush,
and when you'd softly touch my hair
as you'd begin to brush.

And I'd love to feel your heart beat
as you held me close to you,
and learn the many other things
that little girls get to do.

But Momma don't you worry
'cause I love you anyway,
even though I was aborted
when I was almost born today.

HOW TO BECOME A CHRISTIAN

❧ ❧ ❧

GOD HAS ALWAYS WANTED A PERSONAL RELATIONSHIP WITH YOU...

Even before He created you, He chose to show His love toward you, through His sacrifice on the cross, and through His Word. Here are some very simple steps for understanding salvation and becoming a Christian believer.

ADMIT TO GOD THAT YOU HAVE SINNED

The fact is, everyone sins. We need to understand this before we can go any further.

Roman 3:23

"For all have sinned and come short of the glory of God"

Romans 3:10-12

"As it is written: `There is no one righteous, not even one; there is no one who understands, no one who seeks God. All have turned away, they have together become worthless; there is no one who does good, not even one.'"

Unfortunately, there are consequences for our sins. It is death. We all face physical death but anyone who is not a Christian believer when he/she dies, will die spiritually as well as physically and be eternally separated from God.

Romans 6:23a

"The wages of sin is death . . . "

It's also important to know that we cannot earn salvation based on our own merits. We cannot be good enough, or smart enough, or kind enough, or religious enough. We are not only sinners, but we fall short of the standard God requires.

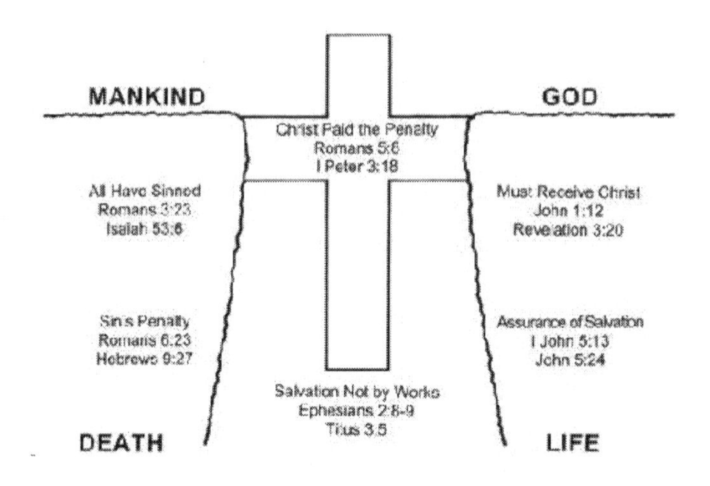

SO, WHAT SHOULD WE DO?

BELIEVE THAT JESUS PAID FOR YOUR SINS ON THE CROSS

When Jesus died on the cross and rose again, He paid the full penalty for your sins and mine, and the sins of every person, living, dead, and even yet unborn. The only condition for receiving His salvation is that we *believe* He did this for us, according to His Word. Yes, He did it because He loves us, and because we couldn't pay for our sins, ourselves.

John 3:16 King James Version (KJV)

"For God so loved the world, that he gave his only begotten Son, that whosoever believeth in him should not perish, but have everlasting life."

Romans 5:8

"God demonstrated His love toward us in that while we were still sinners, Christ died for us."

God's word leads us to believe in Jesus Christ as God's Son and accept Jesus' gift of forgiveness for our sins. Along with God's forgiveness, we will receive God's gift of eternal life.

Romans 6:23b
" . . . the gift of God is Eternal Life through
Jesus Christ our Lord"

Would you like to receive Jesus Christ into your heart
and become a Christian believer today?

Maybe you need some help; a starting point, perhaps?
Here's an example of how a person could
pray to receive salvation:

THE SINNER'S PRAYER

"Dear God, I know that I have sinned against you and am deserving of punishment. But because you love me so much, you sent your only Son, Jesus Christ, to take the punishment that I deserve. With your help, I place my faith and trust in You as my Savior and Lord. Please forgive me and come into my heart. With your help, I will live for you from this day forward. Thank You for saving me, and for offering me Your wonderful grace. Thank You also for the gift of eternal life! In Jesus' name I pray, Amen!"

In themselves, these words will not save you.
But praying in faith
and believing on Jesus Christ, will!

Romans 10:13
"Whosoever will call on the name of the Lord
shall be saved."

Romans 5:1
"Therefore, since we have been Justified through Faith,
we have Peace with God through our Lord Jesus
Christ."

Romans 8:1
"Therefore, there is now no condemnation
for those who are in Christ Jesus."

John 1:12
"And as many as received Him,
and believed in His name,
to them He gave the power
to become children of God."

Romans 8:38-39
"For I am convinced that neither death nor life,
neither angels nor demons neither the present nor the
future, nor any powers, neither height nor depth,
nor anything else in all creation,
will be able to separate us from the love of God
that is in Christ Jesus our Lord."

Romans 10:9-10
"If you confess with your mouth that Jesus is Lord,
and believe in your heart that
God raised Jesus from the dead,
you shall be saved;
for with the heart man believes unto righteousness,
and with the mouth confession is made unto salvation."

WHAT'S NEXT?
Confess your faith in Jesus Christ
Share your experience with the people in your life
so they may come to know Him too.
Talking about it proves you believe in Him.

* * *

AS A CHRISTIAN BELIEVER,
REMEMBER TO DO THE FOLLOWING:
1. Read your Bible daily
2. Pray to the Lord daily
3. Find and attend
a local Bible believing church

Made in the USA
Columbia, SC
26 October 2021